Freedom Press
GRENADES AND PYROTECHNIC SIGNALS

The Following is a U.S. Army Manual without Copyright released to the General Public.

They are provided for informational purposes only.

ISBN-13: 978-1508812302
ISBN-10: 1508812306

FAIR USE ASSERTION

FM 23-30

GRENADES AND
PYROTECHNIC SIGNALS

PREFACE

The purpose of this manual is to orient soldiers to the functions and descriptions of hand grenades and ground pyrotechnic signals. It provides a reference for the identification and capabilities of various hand grenades and pyrotechnic signals. It also provides a guide for the proper handling and throwing of hand grenades, suggests methods and techniques for the tactical employment of hand grenades, and provides a guide for commanders conducting hand grenade training.

This manual provides information and guidance for operating, using, and training with hand grenades. It is intended for two user groups: (1) *training centers* responsible for introducing and training soldiers to a basic knowledge level and (2) *field units*, *officers*, and *noncommissioned officers* responsible for sustaining basic knowledge level skills and advancing soldier skills in the employment of the hand grenades on the battlefield.

The development of new hand grenades and improvement of existing hand grenades has resulted in many different grenade types within the US inventory. While only a limited number of grenade types are in production today for US Armed Forces, the majority of all hand grenades produced are used by either the armed forces of our allies or countries to which we occasionally provide military assistance. This manual addresses hand grenades common to the US Army. Obsolete hand grenades (the hand grenades less likely to be issued to US Army personnel) are addressed in Appendix E.

The proponent of this publication is Headquarters, TRADOC. Send comments and recommendations on DA Form 2028 directly to Commandant, US Army Infantry School, ATTN: ATSH-IN-S3, Fort Benning, GA 31905-5596; email LusanoH@benning.army.mil.

Unless otherwise stated, whenever the masculine gender is used, both men and women are included.

*FM 3-23-30 (23-30)

FIELD MANUAL
NO. 3-23.30

HEADQUARTERS
DEPARTMENT OF THE ARMY
WASHINGTON, DC, 1 September 2000

CONTENTS

DISTRIBUTION RESTRICTION—Approved for public release; distribution is unlimited.

*This publication supersedes FM 23-30, 27 December 1988.

CHAPTER 1

TYPES OF HAND GRENADES

This chapter describes the various types of hand grenades, their components and mechanical functions, and examples of the grenades used by US forces.

1-1. DESCRIPTION

The hand grenade is a handheld, hand-armed, and hand-thrown weapon. US forces use colored smoke, white smoke, riot-control, special purpose, offensive, and practice hand grenades. Each grenade has a different capability that provides the soldier with a variety of options to successfully complete any given mission. Hand grenades give the soldier the ability to kill enemy soldiers and destroy enemy equipment. Historically, the most important hand grenade has been the fragmentation grenade, which is the soldier's personal indirect weapon system. Offensive grenades are much less lethal than fragmentation grenades on an enemy in the open, but they are very effective against an enemy within a confined space. Smoke and special purpose grenades can be used to signal, screen, control crowds or riots, start fires, or destroy equipment. The hand grenade is thrown by hand; therefore, the range is short and the casualty radius is small. The 4- to5-second delay on the fuze allows the soldier to safely employ the grenade.

1-2. COMPONENTS

The hand grenade is made up of the following components:

   a. **Body**. The body contains filler and, in certain grenades, fragmentation.

   b. **Filler**. The filler is composed of a chemical or explosive substance, which determines the type of hand grenade for employment factors.

   c. **Fuze Assembly**. The fuze causes the grenade to ignite or explode by detonating the filler.

1-3. MECHANICAL FUNCTION

The following is the sequence for the M67 fragmentation hand grenade safety clip insertion and arming.

   a. **Insert the Safety Clip**. All hand grenades do not have safety clips (NSN 1330-00-183-5996). However, safety clips are available through Class V ammunition supply channels for some types of grenades. The safety clip is adaptable to the M26 and M67 series, the MK2, and the M69 practice grenade. The safety clip prevents the safety lever from springing loose even if the safety pin assembly is accidentally removed. The adjustment instructions are illustrated in Figure 1-1. The safety clip installation instructions are as follows:

   (1) Hold the fuzed grenade in the palm of the hand with the pull ring up.

   (2) Insert the small loop at the open end of the safety clip in the slot of the fuze body beneath the safety lever.

   (3) Press the clip across the safety lever until the closed end of the clip touches the safety lever and snaps securely into place around the safety lever.

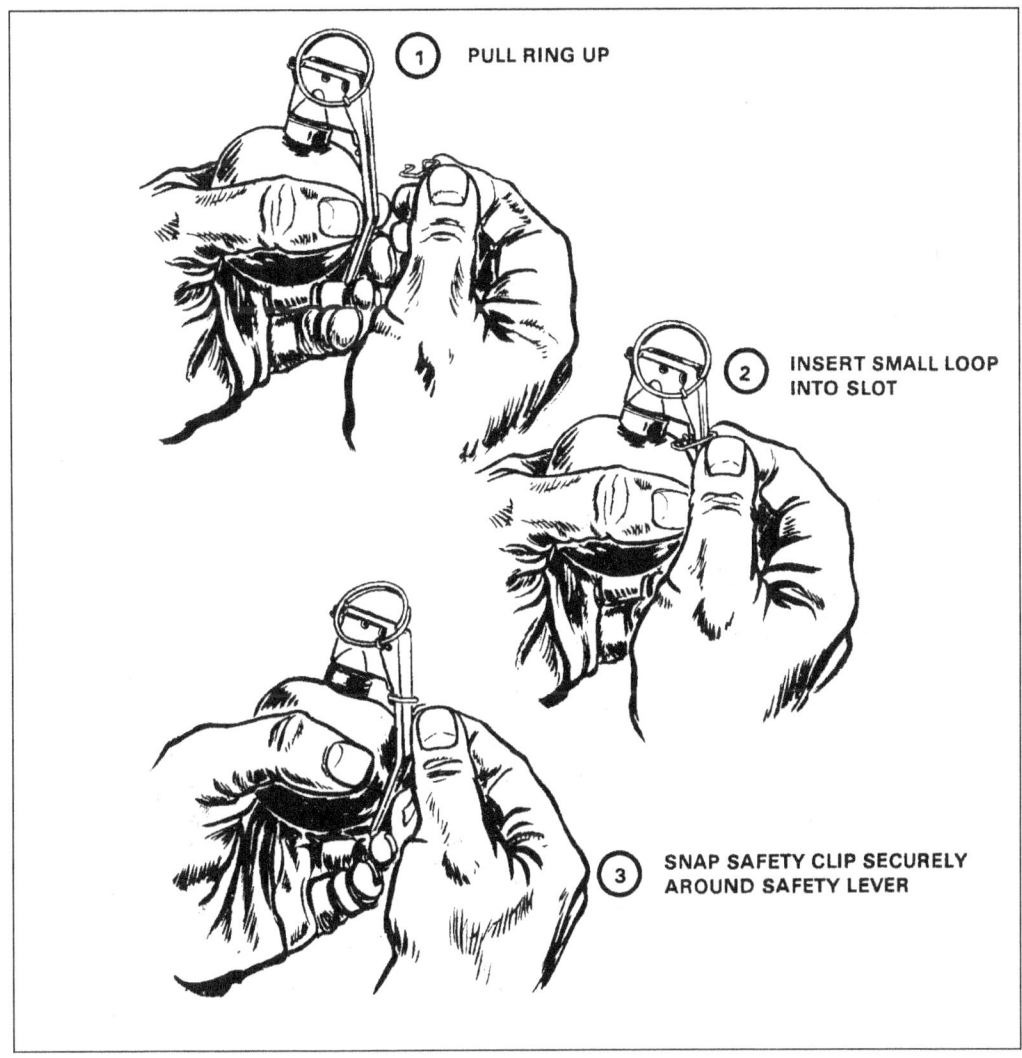

Figure 1-1. Safety clip insertion.

b. **Arming Sequence**. First remove the safety clip, then the safety pin, from the fuze by pulling the pull ring. Be sure to maintain pressure on the safety lever: it springs free once the safety clip and the safety pin assembly are removed.

c. **Release Pressure on Lever**. Once the grenade is thrown, the pressure on the safety lever is released, and the striker is forced to rotate on its axis by the striker spring, throwing the safety lever off. The striker then detonates the primer, and the primer explodes and ignites the delay element. The delay element burns for the prescribed amount of time then activates either the detonator or the igniter. The detonator or igniter acts to either explode or burn the filler substance (Figure 1-2).

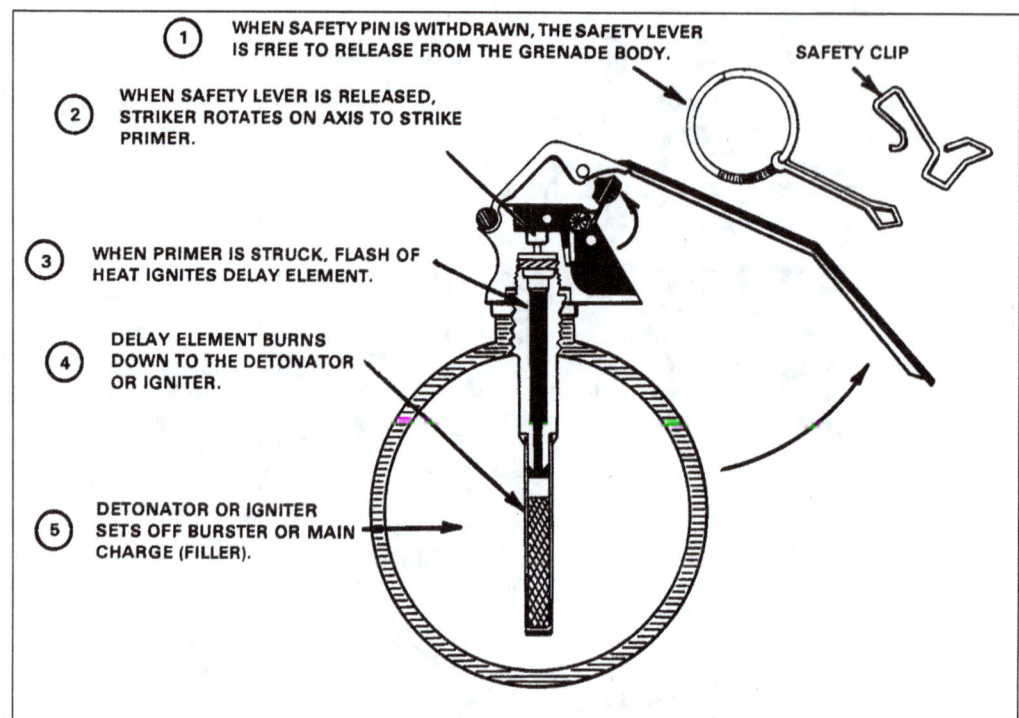

Figure 1-2. Fuze functioning.

1-4. FUZES

The two types of fuzes used in current US hand grenades are detonating and ignition. Both function in the same manner; the difference is how they activate the filler substance.

a. **Detonating Fuze**. Detonating fuzes explode within the grenade body to initiate the main explosion of the filler substance. Detonating fuzes include the M213 and M228.

(1) *M213 fuze*. The M213 fuze (Figure 1-3) is designed for use with the M67 fragmentation grenade. It has a safety clip. The standard delay element is a powder train requiring 4 to 5 seconds to burn to the detonator. In some cases, the delay element may vary from less than 4 seconds to more than 5 seconds due to defective fuzes.

WARNING

If pressure on the safety lever is relaxed after the safety clip and safety pin have been removed, it is possible that the striker can rotate and strike the primer while the thrower is still holding the grenade. This is called "milking" the grenade. Throwers must be instructed to maintain enough pressure on the safety lever so the striker cannot rotate.

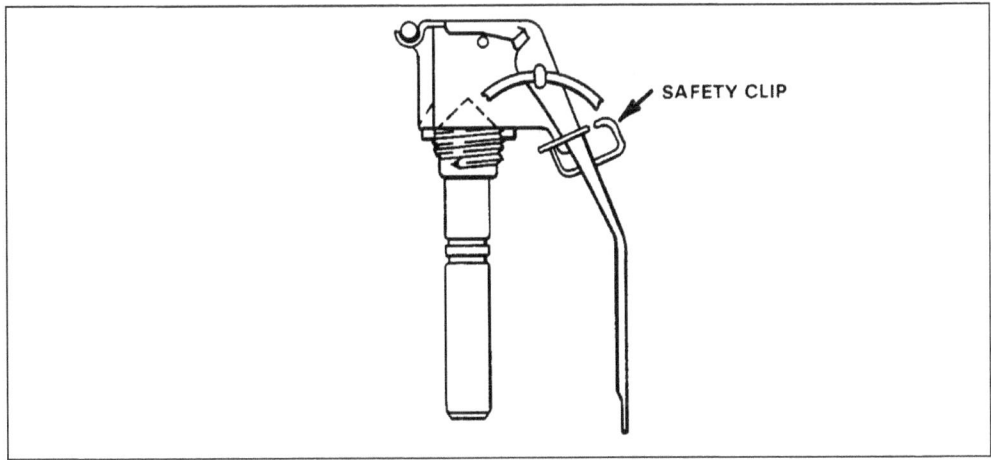

SAFETY CLIP

Figure 1-3. M213 fuze.

(2) *M228 fuze*. The M228 fuze (Figure 1-4) is used with the M69 practice grenade to replicate the fuze delay of the M67 fragmentation hand grenade. The time delay element is a powder train with a 4- to 5-second delay burn. In some cases, however, the delay element may vary from less than 4 seconds to more than 5 seconds due to defective fuzes.

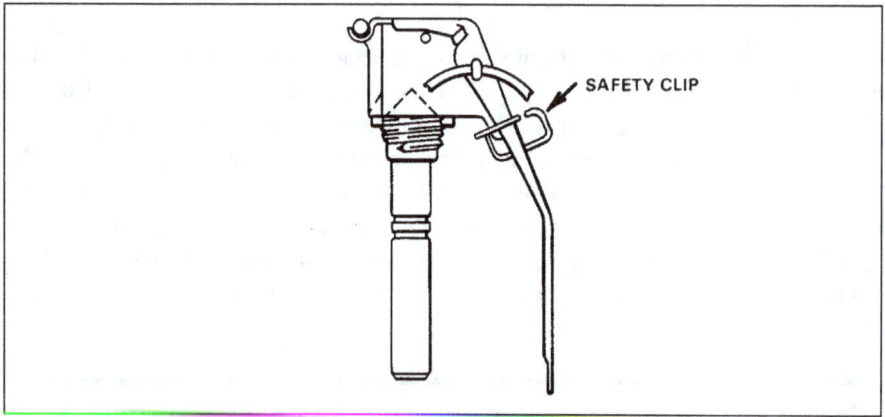

Figure 1-4. M228 fuze.

b. **Igniting Fuze.** Igniting fuzes are designed for use with chemical hand grenades. They burn at high temperatures and ignite the chemical filler. The M201A1 (Figure 1-5) is designed for use with the AN-M83HC white smoke grenade, the AN-M14 TH3 incendiary grenade, and the M18 colored smoke grenade. This fuze is interchangeable with any standard firing device. The time delay element is a powder train requiring 1.2 to 2 seconds to burn to the igniter. The igniter ignites the filler or a pyrotechnic starter with a violent burning action and expels the filler from the grenade body.

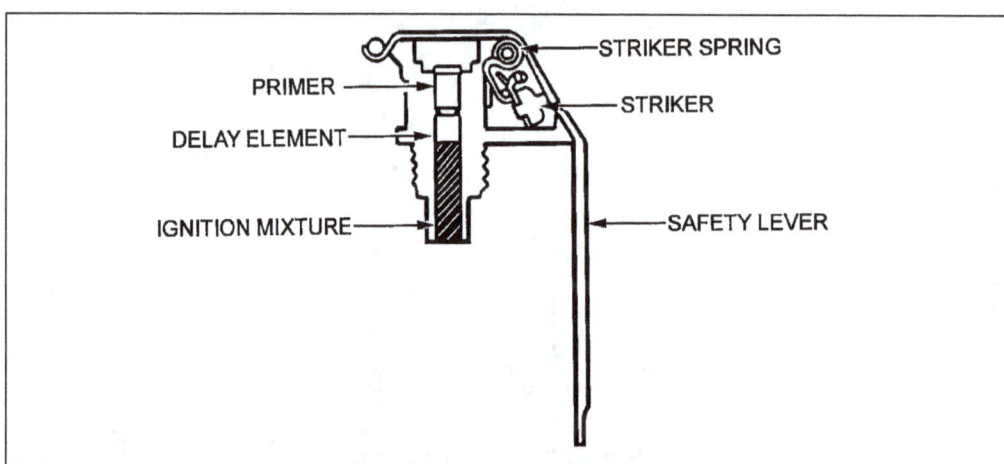

Figure 1-5. M201A1 fuze.

1-5. FRAGMENTATION HAND GRENADES

The following is a description of the M67 fragmentation hand grenade (Figure 1-6):

a. **Body**. The body is a steel sphere.

b. **Filler**. The filler has 6.5 ounces of Composition B.

c. **Fuze**. The fuze is an M213.

d. **Weight**. The grenade weighs 14 ounces.

e. **Safety Clip**. The grenade has a safety clip. (See paragraph 1-3.)

f. **Capabilities**. The average soldier can throw the M67 grenade 35 meters effectively. The effective casualty-producing radius is 15 meters and the killing radius is 5 meters.

g. **Color and Markings**. The grenade has an olive drab body with a single-yellow band at the top. Markings are in yellow.

WARNING
Although the killing radius of this grenade is 5 meters and the casualty-producing radius is 15 meters, fragmentation can disperse as far away as 230 meters.

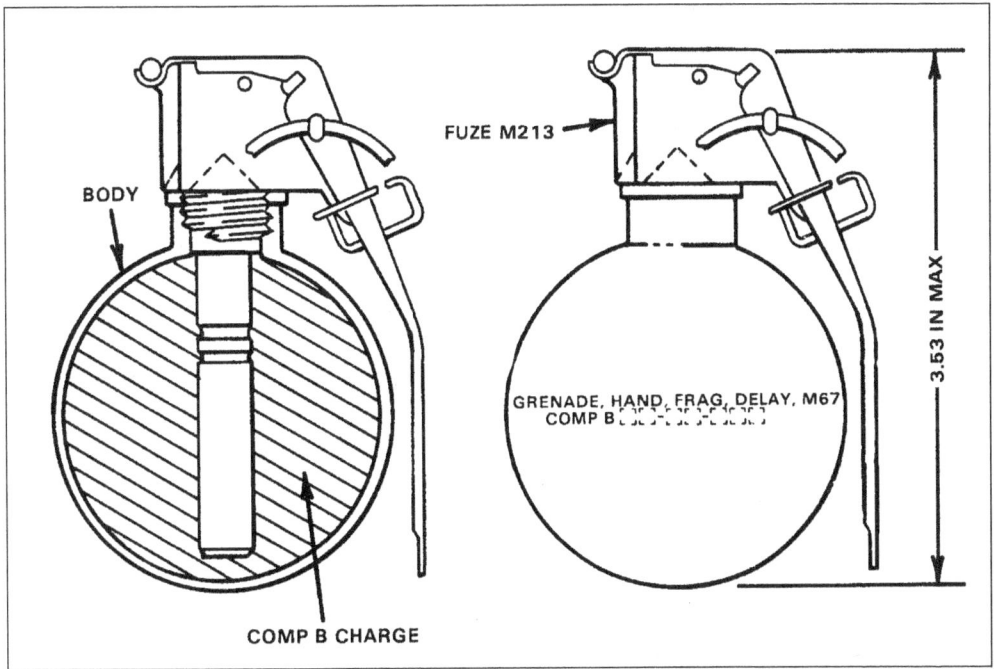

Figure 1-6. M67 fragmentation hand grenade.

1-6. SMOKE HAND GRENADES

Smoke hand grenades are used as ground-to-ground or ground-to-air signaling devices, target or landing zone marking devices, or screening devices for unit movements.

a. **M18 Colored Smoke Hand Grenade**. The following is a description of the M18 colored smoke hand grenade and its components (Figure 1-7).

(1) *Body*. The body has a sheet steel cylinder with four emission holes at the top and one at the bottom. The holes allow smoke to escape when the grenade is ignited.

(2) *Filler*. The filler has 11.5 ounces of colored smoke mixture (red, yellow, green and violet).

(3) *Fuze*. The fuze is an M201A1.

(4) *Weight*. The grenade weighs 19 ounces.

(5) *Safety clip*. This grenade does not have a safety clip.

(6) *Capabilities*. The average soldier can throw this grenade 35 meters. It produces a cloud of colored smoke for 50 to 90 seconds.

(7) *Color and markings*. The grenade has an olive drab body with the top indicating the smoke color.

(8) *Field expedient*. In combat, you may need to use the M18 hand grenade without the fuze. Use the following procedures *in combat only*:

- Remove the tape from the grenade bottom to expose the filler.
- Remove the fuze by unscrewing it from the grenade.
- Ignite the starter mixture with an open flame.
- Throw the grenade immediately to avoid burn injury.

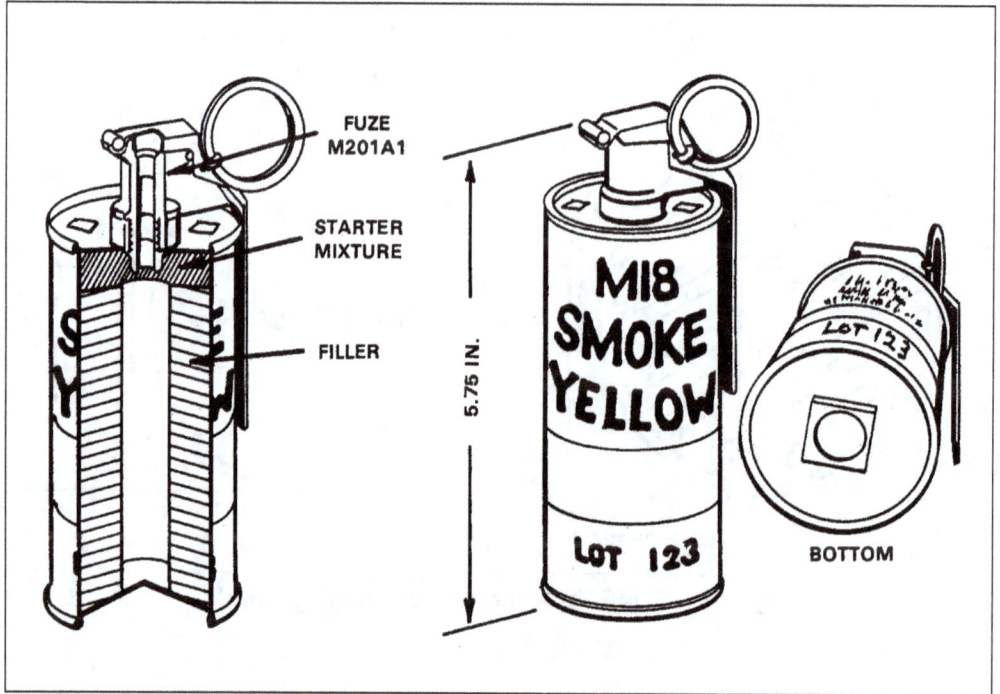

Figure 1-7. M18 colored smoke hand grenade.

WARNING

Do not use a smoke grenade in an enclosed area. If you must remain in the area with the smoke, always wear a protective mask.

---

b. **AN-M83 HC White Smoke Hand Grenade.** The AN-M83 HC white smoke hand grenade (Figure 1-8) is used for screening the activities of small units and for ground-to-air signaling.

(1) *Body.* The body is a cylinder of thin sheet metal, 2.5 inches in diameter.

(2) *Filler.* The filler has 11 ounces of terephthalic acid.

(3) *Fuze.* The fuze is an M201A1.

(4) *Weight.* The grenade weighs 16 ounces and is 2.5 inches in diameter and 5.7 inches in length.

(5) *Safety clip.* This grenade does not have a safety clip.

(6) *Capabilities.* The AN-M83 produces a cloud of white smoke for 25 to 70 seconds.

(7) *Color and markings.* The grenade has a forest green body with light green markings, a blue band, and a white top.

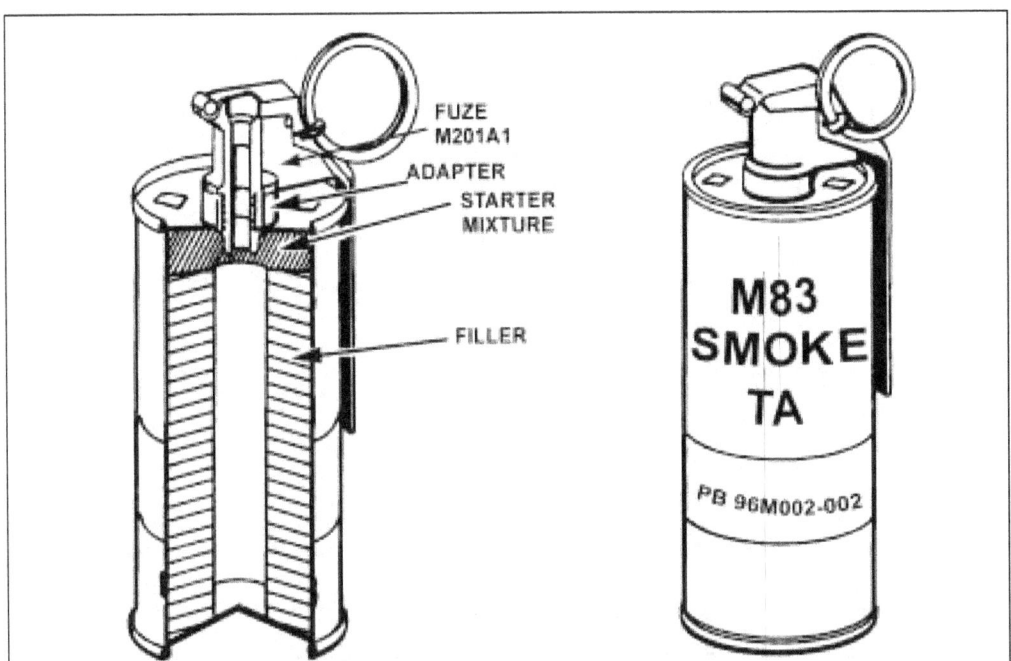

Figure 1-8. AN-M83 white smoke hand grenade.

1-7. RIOT-CONTROL HAND GRENADES

The ABC-M7A2 and ABC-M7A3 riot-control hand grenades (Figure 1-9) contain only CS as a filler. They differ only in the amount of filler and the form of the CS they contain. Description and components are as follows:

a. **Body**. The bodies of both grenades are sheet metal with four emission holes at the top and one at the bottom.

b. **Filler**. The ABC-7A2 grenade has 5.5 ounces of burning mixture and 3.5 ounces of CS in gelatin capsules. The ABC-M7A3 has 7.5 ounces of burning mixture and 4.5 ounces of pelletized CS agent.

c. **Fuze**. The fuze for either grenade is an M201A1.

d. **Weight**. Each grenade weighs about 15.5 ounces.

e. **Safety**. These grenades do not have safety clips.

f. **Capabilities**. The average soldier can throw these grenades 40 meters. Both grenades produce a cloud of irritant agent for 15 to 35 seconds.

g. **Color and Markings**. Both grenades have gray bodies with red bands and markings.

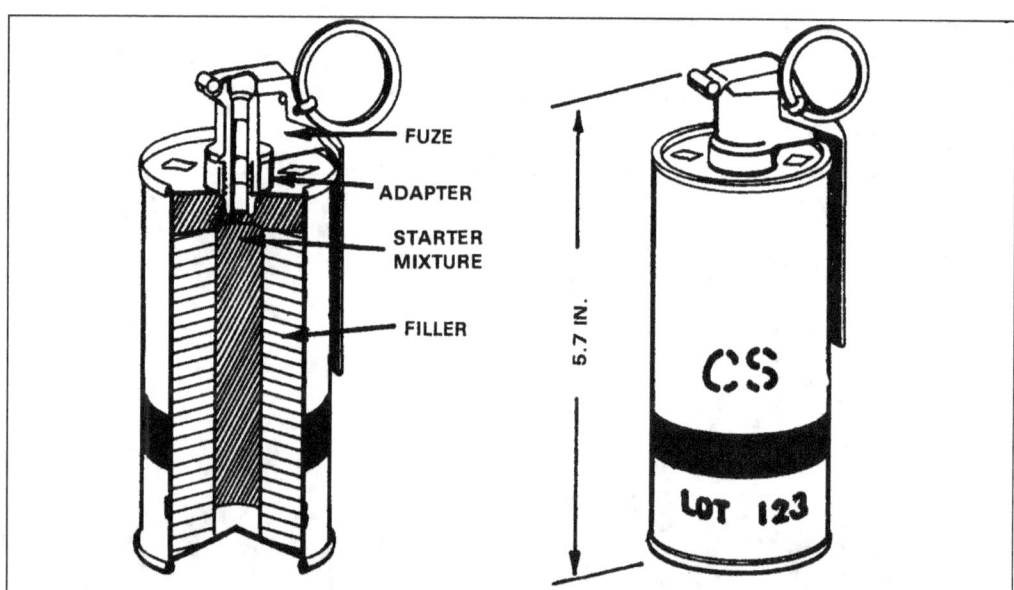

Figure 1-9. ABC-M7A2 and M7A3 riot-control hand grenades.

WARNING

Do not use a riot control grenade in an enclosed area. If you must remain in the area, always wear a protective mask.

1-8. SPECIAL-PURPOSE HAND GRENADES

a. **Incendiary**. The AN-M14 TH3 incendiary hand grenade (Figure 1-10) is used to destroy equipment or start fires. It can also damage, immobilize, or destroy vehicles, weapons systems, shelters, or munitions. The description and components are as follows:

(1) *Body*. The body is sheet metal.

(2) *Filler*. The filler has 26.5 ounces of thermate (TH3) mixture.

(3) *Fuze*. The fuze is an M201A1.

(4) *Weight*. The grenade weighs 32 ounces.

(5) *Safety clip*. This grenade does not have a safety clip.

(6) *Capabilities*. The average soldier can throw this grenade 25 meters. A portion of thermate mixture is converted to molten iron, which burns at 4,000 degrees Fahrenheit. The mixture fuzes together the metallic parts of any object that it contacts. Thermate is an improved version of thermite, the incendiary agent used in hand grenades during World War II. The thermate filler can burn through a 1/2-inch homogenous steel plate. It produces its own oxygen and burns under water.

(7) *Color and markings*. The grenade is gray in color with purple markings and a single purple band (current grenades). Under the standard color-coding system, incendiary grenades are light red with black markings.

WARNING

Avoid looking directly at the incendiary hand grenade as it burns. The intensity of the light is hazardous to the retina and can cause permanent eye damage.

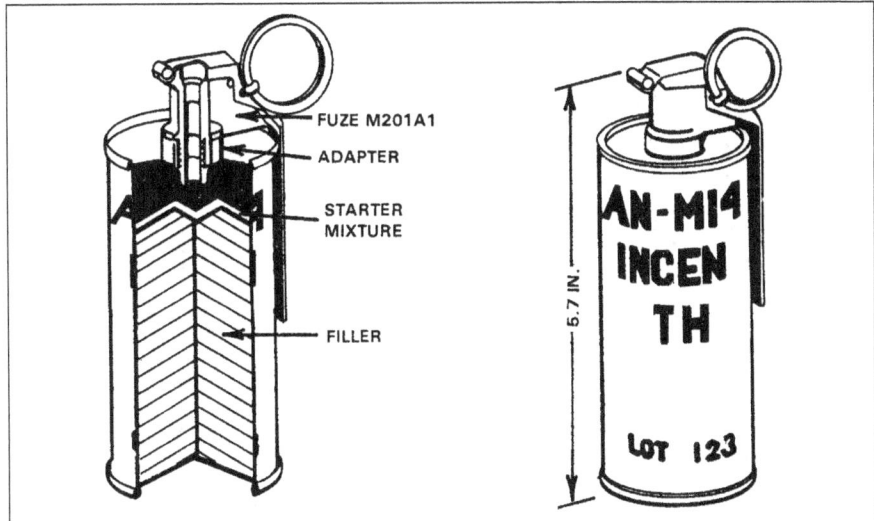

Figure 1-10. AN-M14 TH3 incendiary hand grenade.

b. **Offensive**. The MK3A2 offensive hand grenade (Figure 1-11), commonly referred to as the concussion grenade, is designed to produce casualties during close combat while minimizing danger to friendly personnel. The grenade is also used for concussion effects in enclosed areas, for blasting, and for demolition tasks. The shock waves (overpressure) produced by this grenade when used in enclosed areas are greater than those produced by the fragmentation grenade. It is, therefore, very effective against enemy soldiers located in bunkers, buildings, and fortified areas.

(1) *Body*. The body is fiber (similar to the packing container for the fragmentation grenade.)

(2) *Filler*. The filler has 8 ounces of TNT.

(3) *Fuze*. The fuze is an M206A1 or M206A2 (see paragraph 1-4).

(4) *Weight*. The grenade weighs 15.6 ounces.

(5) *Safety clip*. The MK3A2 may be issued with or without a safety clip (see paragraph 1-3).

(6) *Capabilities*. The average soldier can throw this grenade 40 meters. It has an effective casualty radius of 2 meters in open areas, but secondary missiles and bits of fuze may be projected as far as 200 meters from the detonation point.

(7) *Color and markings*. The grenade is black with yellow markings around its middle.

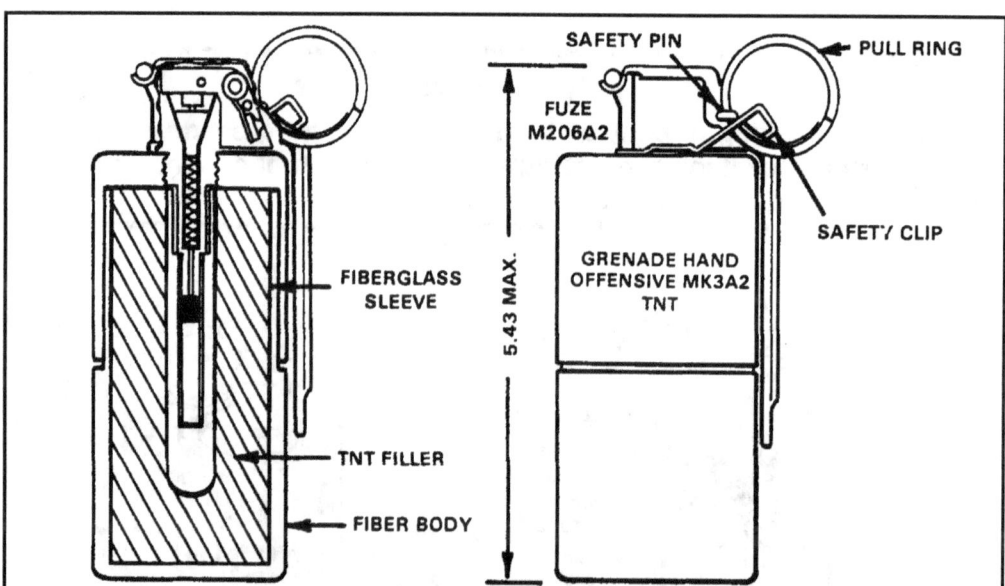

Figure 1-11. MK3A2 offensive grenade.

1-9. PRACTICE HAND GRENADES

The M69 practice hand grenade (Figure 1-12) simulates the M67 series of fragmentation hand grenades for training purposes. The grenade provides realistic training and familiarizes the soldier with the functioning and characteristics of the fragmentation hand grenade. The following is a description of the M69 practice hand grenade and its components:

a. **Body**. The body is a steel sphere.

b. **Fuze**. The fuze is an M228, which is inserted into the grenade body.

c. **Weight**. The grenade weighs 14 ounces.

d. **Safety Clip**. The M69 grenade has a safety clip.

e. **Capabilities**. The average soldier can throw the M69 hand grenade 40 meters. After a delay of 4 to 5 seconds, the M69 emits a small puff of white smoke and makes a loud popping noise. The grenade body can be used repeatedly by replacing the fuze assembly.

f. **Color and Markings**. The grenade is light blue with white markings. The safety lever of the fuze is light blue with black markings and a brown tip.

WARNING
Fuze fragments may exit the hole in the base of the grenade body and cause injuries.

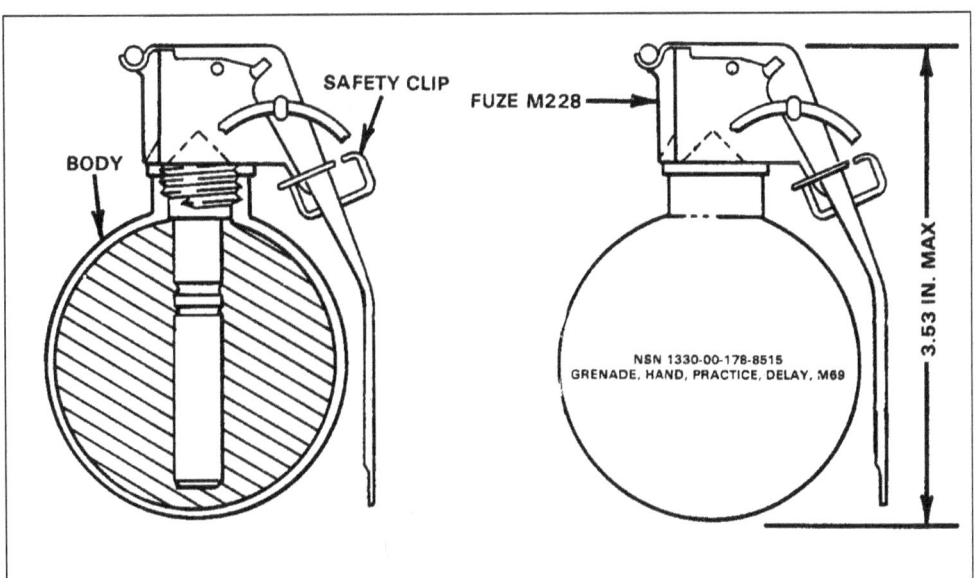

Figure 1-12. M69 practice hand grenade.

1-10. STUN HAND GRENADES

Stun hand grenades are used as diversionary or distraction devices during building and room clearing operations when the presence of noncombatants is likely or expected and the assaulting element is attempting to achieve surprise. The following is a description of the M84 diversionary/flash-bang stun hand grenade and its components (Figure 1-13).

a. **Body**. The body is a steel hexagon tube with holes along the sides to allow for the emission of intense light and sound when the grenade is ignited.

b. **Fuze and safety pin**. The fuze is the M201A1. The M84 also has a secondary safety pin with a triangular pull ring.

c. **Weight**. The grenade weighs 8.33 ounces.

d. **Capabilities**. The handheld device is designed to be thrown into a room (through an open door, a standard glass window, or other opening) where it delivers a loud bang and bright flash sufficient to temporarily disorient personnel in the room.

e. **Field-expedient early warning device**. In combat, you may need to use the M84 stun hand grenade as an early warning device. Use the following procedures <u>in combat only</u>:

(1) Attach the grenade to a secure object such as a tree, post, or picket.

(2) Attach a tripwire to a secure object, extend it across a path, and attach it to the pull ring of the grenade.

(3) Bend the end of the pull pin flat to allow for easy pulling.

(4) Remove the secondary safety pin.

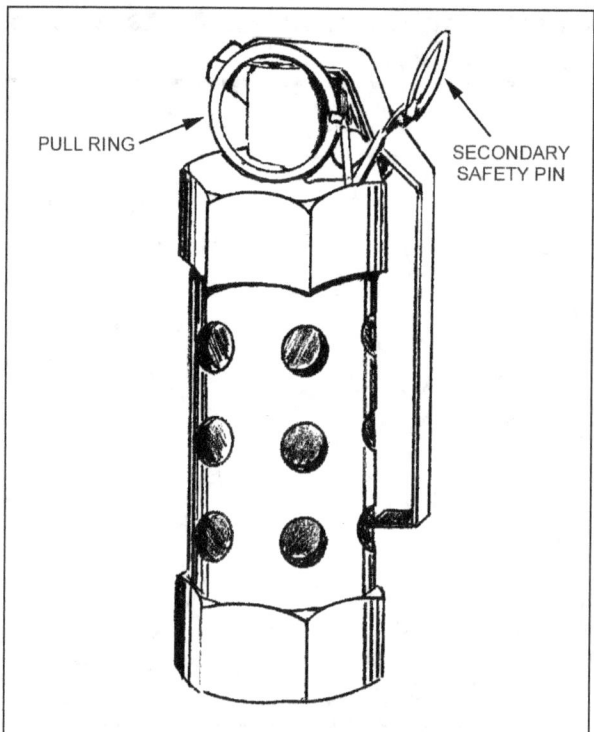

Figure 1-13. M84 stun hand grenade.

CAUTION

Use stun grenades as field-expedient early warning devices only when in a combat environment.

CHAPTER 2
MAINTENANCE

Proper maintenance contributes to a weapon's effectiveness as well as a unit's readiness. This chapter discusses the maintenance aspects of all hand grenades within the US inventory to include inspection, cleaning, lubrication, and maintenance before throwing live or practice hand grenades.

2-1. GENERAL ASSEMBLY

Hand grenades within the US inventory are composed of a body and a fuze. Most hand grenades come assembled with the exception of the M69 practice hand grenade and the fuzes for the M69, which come in flats of 45 fuzes.

2-2. INSPECTION PROCEDURES

Hand grenades within the US inventory are specifically designed and manufactured to overcome any situation during combat or training missions. Grenades can be used to save or take lives. Hand grenades are simple yet powerful weapons used in combat or any training mission. As simple as they may seem, however, hand grenades—like any other weapon—must be inspected before use in order to avoid serious injury or death. The following inspection procedures apply to all hand grenades within the US inventory.

   a. **Newly Issued Hand Grenades**.

   (1) Remove the tape and the top cover from the shipping canister.

   (2) Look down into the canister; if the hand grenade is upside down, return the canister to the issuing person (NCOIC or OIC).

   (3) Ensure all required safeties are properly attached to the hand grenade. If a safety pin is missing, return it.

   (4) Check the hand grenade for rust on the body or the fuze. If it has rusted, return it.

   (5) Check for holes on the body and the fuze. If any holes are visible, return the hand grenade.

   (6) If the hand grenade seems to be in order, remove the grenade carefully from the canister and make a visual check for proper fitting of the safety pins. Then, properly secure the grenade to the ammunition pouch.

   b. **Grenades That Are Unpacked or Stored on Ammunition Pouches**.

   (1) Inspect unpacked grenades daily to ensure safety pins are present. Under hostile conditions, the safety clip must be removed from the fragmentation hand grenade since soldiers under stressful situations sometimes forget to remove the clip when throwing the grenade.

   (2) Check the body for rust or dirt.

   (3) Make sure the lever is not broken or bent.

2-3. CLEANING, LUBRICATION, AND PREVENTIVE MAINTENANCE

Hand grenades are like any other weapon; they must be inspected and cleaned weekly when exposed to the environment. The body of the hand grenade is made of metal, which rusts when it is exposed to moisture or submerged in water. If not removed, dirt or rust can cause the hand grenade to malfunction.

a. **Cleaning**. Wipe the dirt off the body of the hand grenade using a slightly damp cloth or a light brush. For the fuze head, a light brush is recommended since it can reach into the crevices.

b. **Lubrication**. Depending on weather conditions, a light coat of CLP may be needed.

c. **Preventive Maintenance**. For most hand grenades, keeping them clean and lubricated is sufficient maintenance. With the M69 practice grenade, however, maintenance is more difficult since the bodies are used repeatedly. The M69 practice grenade must be cleaned with a wire brush and painted at least quarterly. The threads must be cleaned with a wire brush on a monthly basis, and fuze residue must be removed from the body immediately after each use. Cleaning the threads and removing the residue from the hand grenade body make replacement of the fuzes easier. The grenade body lasts longer if these preventive maintenance procedures are performed.

CHAPTER 3
EMPLOYMENT OF HAND GRENADES

This chapter addresses the fundamentals that develop a soldier's skill and confidence in hand grenade use. These fundamentals include proper carrying, proper handgrips, and the three basic hand grenade throwing techniques. This chapter explains how effective and versatile the hand grenade is and how easily it can be carried. The tactical employment of hand grenades is limited only by the imagination of the user. With confidence and good training, soldiers can put this small but powerful weapon to good use against enemy forces or in any training environment.

Section I. INTRODUCTION TO HAND GRENADE TRAINING

The rifle, the bayonet, and the hand grenade are the soldier's basic lethal weapons. Historically, hand grenade training has received less emphasis than marksmanship and bayonet training. The hand grenade must receive greater emphasis in training programs and field training exercises. The proper use of hand grenades could determine the fate of the soldier or the success of the mission.

Leaders at all levels should study the employment of grenades in conjunction with the unit mission and implement a training program that supports that mission. Once soldiers can safely arm and throw live fragmentation grenades, units should integrate the use of grenades into collective tasks, rather than training these skills as a separate event. Hand grenades must be integrated with other available weapons systems to enhance the unit's combat power on the modern battlefield. We must conduct hand grenade training in the same manner in which we plan to fight.

We cannot let the danger associated with hand grenades deter our training efforts. Proper control and safety procedures allow us to conduct hand grenade training in a safe manner. Train soldiers to standard, and safety is inherent.

Hand grenades include more than casualty-producing instruments of war. They are used to signal, screen, and control crowds. The current inventory provides a specific hand grenade for most circumstances. Soldiers must be familiar with current grenades, their descriptions, and how best to employ each.

3-1. HAND GRENADE STORING

The storing of hand grenades on ammunition pouches is one of the most neglected aspects of hand grenade training. Experiences of American infantry, both in combat and in training, point out the need for specific training in storing hand grenades on ammunition pouches and integration of this type of training into tactical training exercises. Commanders should make every effort to issue training hand grenades for wear and use during all training activities. The soldier must be as confident in carrying and using hand grenades as he is with his rifle and bayonet. Before storing a hand grenade, take the following safety precautions:

a. Check the grenade fuze assembly for tightness. It must be tightly fitted in the grenade fuze well to prevent the grenade from working loose and separating from the grenade body. Never remove the fuze from a grenade.

b. If the grenade safety lever is broken, do not use the grenade. A broken safety lever denies the thrower the most critical safety mechanism of the grenade.

c. Do not bend the ends of the safety pin back flush against the fuze body. This practice, intended to preclude the accidental pulling of the pin, makes the removal of the safety pin difficult. Repeated working of the safety pin in this manner causes the pin to break, creating a hazardous condition.

d. Carry hand grenades either on the ammunition pouch, using the carrying safety straps that designed specifically for this purpose (Figure 3-1), or in the grenade pockets of the enhanced tactical load-bearing vest (Figure 3-2).

(1) *Standard ammunition pouch.* Open the web carrying sleeve on the side of the ammunition pouch and slide the grenade into the sleeve with the safety lever against the side of the ammunition pouch. Be sure the pull ring is in the downward position. Wrap the carrying strap around the neck of the fuze and snap the carrying strap to the carrying sleeve.

Figure 3-1. Standard ammunition pouch.

(2) *Enhanced tactical load-bearing vest.* The enhanced tactical load-bearing vest (ETLBV) has slanted pockets for carrying hand grenades. The grenades are not exposed and are safer to carry than in the standard ammunition pouch. The ETLBV is intended to provide the combat soldier with a comfortable and efficient method of transporting the individual fighting load.

- **Description**. The ETLBV has permanently attached ammunition and grenade pockets. The vest is compatible with the standard equipment belt. It incorporates adjustments to allow for proper fitting.
- **Components materials**. The ETLBV has 7 yards and 5 ounces of nylon fabric and nylon webbing.
- **Color**. The coloring of the ETLBV is woodland camouflage.
- **Weight**. The ETLBV weighs 1.9 pounds.

- **Size**. The ETLBV comes in one size that fits all.
- **Basis of issue**. Each infantry soldier should receive one ETLBV.

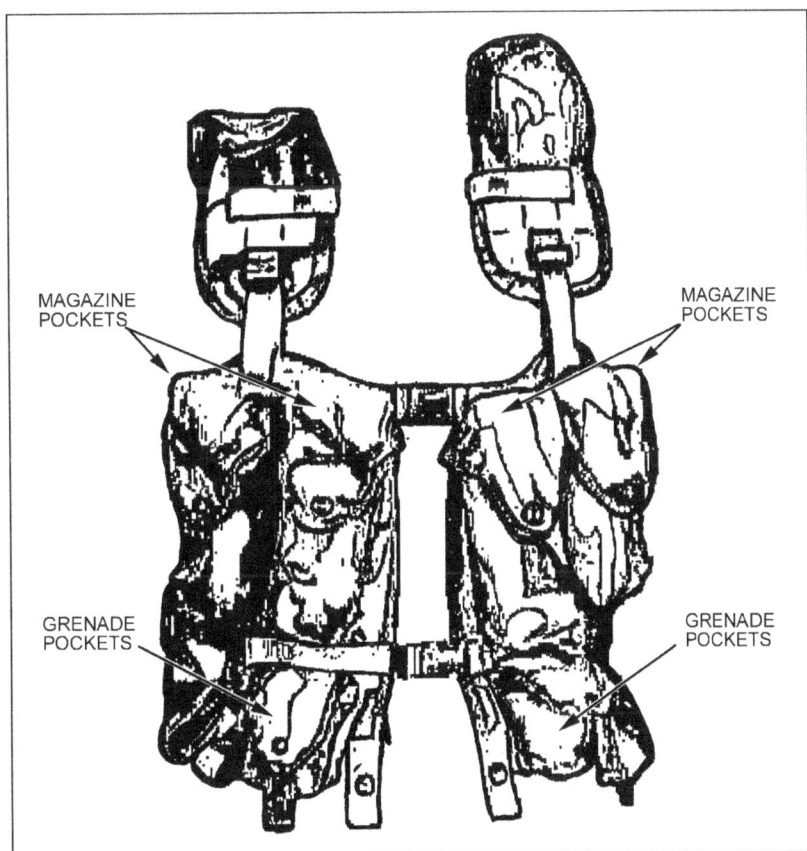

Figure 3-2. Enhanced tactical load-bearing vest.

3-2. HAND GRENADE GRIPPING PROCEDURES

The importance of properly gripping the hand grenade cannot be overemphasized. Soldiers must understand that a grenade not held properly is difficult to arm. Sustainment training is the key to maintaining grip efficiency. Gripping procedures differ slightly for right- and left-handed soldiers:

a. Holding the grenade in the throwing hand with the safety lever placed between the first and second joints of the thumb provides safety and throwing efficiency.

b. Right-handed soldiers hold the grenade upright with the pull ring away from the palm of the throwing hand so that the pull ring can be easily removed by the index or middle finger of the free hand (Figure 3-3).

c. Left-handed soldiers invert the grenade with the fingers and thumb of the throwing hand positioned in the same manner as by right-handed personnel (Figure 3-4).

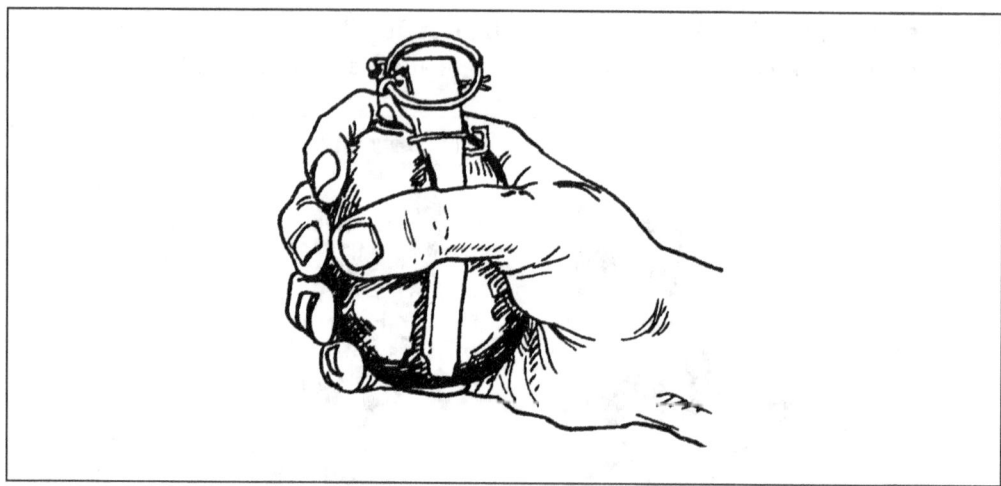

Figure 3-3. Right-handed grip.

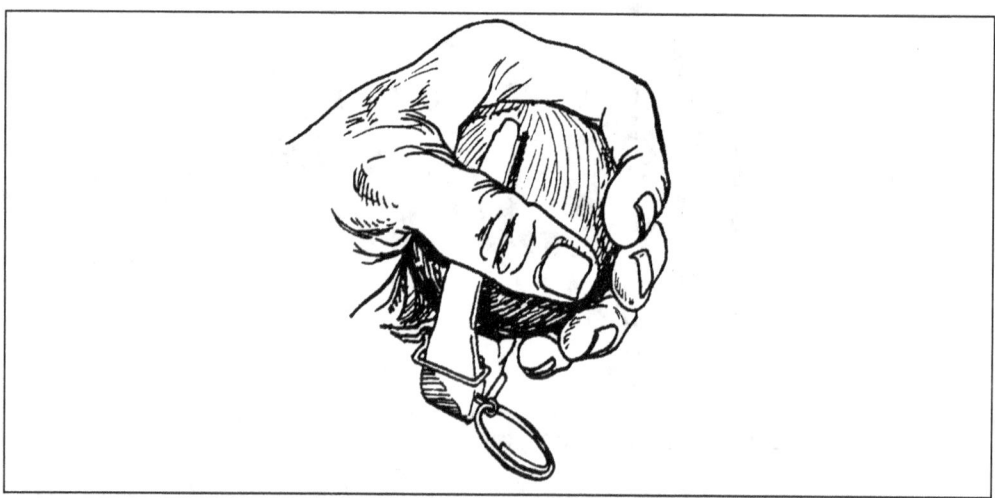

Figure 3-4. Left-handed grip.

3-3. HAND GRENADE THROWING

Since few soldiers throw in the same manner, it is difficult to establish firm rules or techniques for throwing hand grenades. How accurately they are thrown is more important than how they are thrown. If a soldier can achieve more distance and accuracy using his own personal style, he should be allowed to do so as long as his body is facing sideways, towards the enemy's position, and he throws basically overhand. There is, however, a recommended method of throwing hand grenades.

a. **Employ Grenades**. Use the following procedures:

(1) Observe the target to mentally establish the distance between your throwing position and the target area. In observing the target, minimize your exposure time to the enemy (no more than 3 seconds).

(2) Grip the hand grenade in your throwing hand.

(3) Grasp the pull ring with the index or middle finger of your nonthrowing hand. Remove the safety pin with a pulling and twisting motion. If the tactical situation permits, observe the safety pin's removal.

(4) Look at the target and throw the grenade using the overhand method so that the grenade arcs, landing on or near the target.

(5) Allow the motion of your throwing arm to continue naturally once you release the grenade. This follow-through improves distance and accuracy and lessens the strain on your throwing arm.

(6) Practice the necessary throws that are used in combat, such as the underhand and sidearm throws. Soldiers can practice these throws with practice grenades, but they must throw live fragmentation grenades overhand in a training environment.

b. **Throwing Positions**. In training, throwing positions are used for uniformity, control, and to familiarize soldiers with the proper manner of throwing grenades in combat if the situation gives you a choice. Consider the following throwing positions when employing grenades:

(1) *Standing*. The standing position (Figure 3-5) is the most desirable and natural position from which to throw grenades. It allows you to obtain the greatest possible throwing distance. Soldiers normally use this position when occupying a fighting position or during operations in fortified positions or urban terrain. Use the following procedures when throwing from this position:

(a) Observe the target to mentally estimate the distance. Use the proper handgrip and arm the grenade while behind cover.

(b) Assume a natural stance with your weight balanced equally on both feet. Hold the grenade shoulder high and hold the nonthrowing hand at a 45-degree angle with the fingers and thumb extended, joined, and pointing toward the intended target.

(c) Throw the grenade with a natural motion, using the procedures described in paragraph 3-3.

(d) Seek cover to avoid being hit by fragments or direct enemy fire. If no cover is available, drop to the prone position with your Kevlar facing the direction of the grenade's detonation.

Figure 3-5. Standing throwing position.

(2) *Kneeling*. The kneeling position (Figure 3-6) reduces the distance a soldier can throw a grenade. It is used primarily when a soldier has only a low wall, a shallow ditch, or similar cover to protect him. Use the following procedures when throwing from this position:

(a) Observe the target to mentally estimate the throwing distance. Using the proper grip, arm the grenade while behind cover.

(b) Hold the grenade shoulder high and bend your nonthrowing knee at a 90-degree angle, placing that knee on the ground. Keep your throwing leg straight and locked, with the side of your boot firmly on the ground. Move your body to face sideways toward the target position. Keep your nonthrowing hand at a 45-degree angle with your fingers and thumb extended, joined, and pointing toward the enemy position.

(c) Throw the grenade with a natural throwing motion. Push off with your throwing foot to give added force to your throw. Follow through with your throwing arm as described in paragraph 3-3.

(d) Drop to the prone position or behind available cover to reduce exposure to fragmentation and direct enemy fire.

Figure 3-6. Kneeling throwing position.

(3) *Alternate prone.* The alternate prone position (Figure 3-7) reduces both distance and accuracy. It is used only when an individual is pinned down by hostile fire and is unable to rise to engage his target. Use the following procedures when throwing from this position:

(a) Lie down on your back with your body parallel to the grenade's intended line of flight. Hold the grenade at chin-chest level and remove the safety pins.

(b) Cock your throwing leg at a 45-degree angle, maintaining knee-to-knee contact and bracing the side of your boot firmly on the ground. Hold the grenade 4 to 6 inches behind your ear with your arm cocked for throwing.

(c) With your free hand, grasp any object that is capable of giving added leverage to increase your throwing distance. In throwing the grenade, push off with your rearward foot to give added force to your throw. Do not lift your head or body when attempting to throw a grenade as this exposes you to direct enemy fire.

(d) After throwing the grenade, roll over onto your stomach and press flat against the ground.

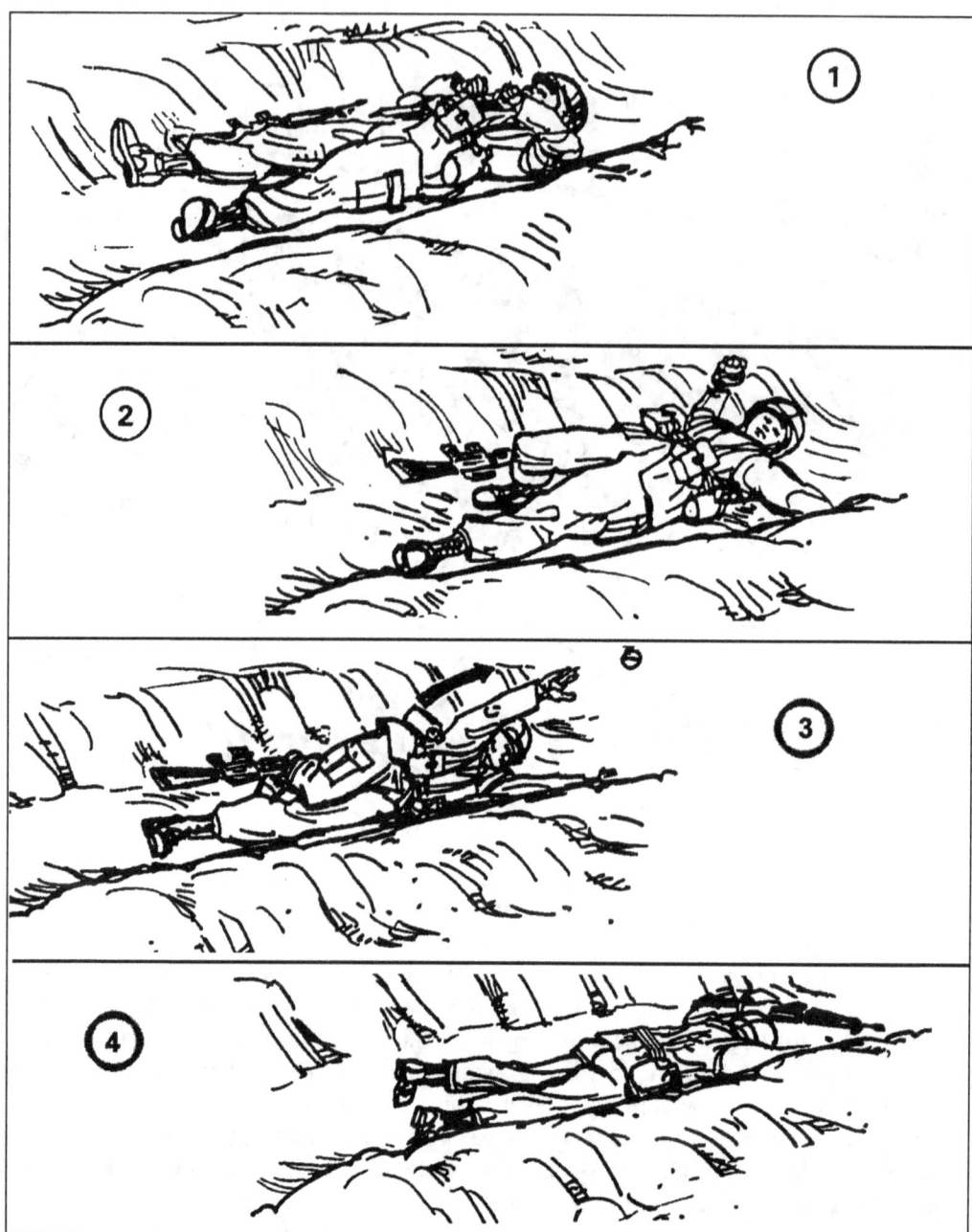

Figure 3-7. Alternate prone throwing position.

Section II. TACTICAL EMPLOYMENT

Hand grenades provide the individual soldier with a number of highly versatile and effective weapons systems. Soldiers employ hand grenades throughout the spectrum of warfare, from low to high intensity conflict, to prevent giving away positions, to save ammunition, and to inflict greater casualties.

3-4. APPLICATION

Soldiers use hand grenades in defensive missions, offensive missions, and retrograde operations. All soldiers use hand grenades during close, deep, and rear operations, during all conditions of combat, and in all types of terrain. Hand grenades have the following specific applications:

- Fragmentation hand grenades are mainly used to kill or wound enemy soldiers but can also be used to destroy or disable equipment.
- Incendiary hand grenades are mainly used to destroy equipment and start fires but can also be used to destroy or disable vehicles and weapons.
- Colored smoke is mainly used to identify or mark positions but can also be used to mark areas for ground-to-ground operations or ground-to-air operations.
- White smoke is mainly used to conceal or create a smoke screen for offensive or retrograde operations.
- Riot-control hand grenades are used to control crowds or riots.
- Stun grenades are used to temporarily stun or disorient the occupants of an enclosed area such as a building or room.

While all hand grenades have application in modern combat, the fragmentation hand grenade remains the most important because it is not only the primary killing hand grenade but also the most dangerous to employ. Fragmentation hand grenades are equally lethal to friendly and enemy soldiers; therefore, we must employ them properly to protect our own soldiers.

3-5. CLOSE COMBAT

On the modern battlefield, the close-in fight can occur anywhere, anytime. The rifle, bayonet, and hand grenade are basic weapons of warfare for the individual soldier. The rifle gives the soldier the ability to kill enemy soldiers with direct fire out to the maximum effective line-of-sight range. Fragmentation hand grenades, on the other hand, allow the soldier to effectively engage and kill enemy soldiers located within a radius of 40 meters where line-of-sight systems, including the rifle, are no longer effective. Since there is no muzzle flash, grenades also help conceal a soldier's position as he engages the enemy. While the rifle is the safest and most discriminating weapon at close ranges, the fragmentation hand grenade is the weapon of choice when the enemy is within range but the terrain masks engagement areas. The fragmentation hand grenade is the soldier's indirect-fire weapon system.

a. Many times in combat, the nature of the targets confronting the infantryman make normal methods of target engagement inadequate. Against soldiers or weapons in trenches or fighting positions, for example, having a grenade burst over the target is more effective. Furthermore, if the targets are on sloping ground, then a grenade needs to detonate as near impact as possible to prevent its rolling away from the target before detonating. Such aboveground detonation also prevents the enemy from securing the grenade and throwing it back within the 4- to 5-second fuze delay.

b. Aboveground detonation is especially critical when engaging bunker-type emplacements. To achieve aboveground detonation or near-impact detonation, remove the grenade's safety pin, release the safety lever, count ONE THOUSAND ONE, ONE THOUSAND TWO, and throw the grenade. This is called *cooking-off*. Cooking-off expends a sufficient period (about 2 seconds) of the grenade's 4- to 5-second delay. This causes the grenade to detonate above ground or shortly after impact with the target. Do not cook-off fragmentation or white phosphorous hand grenades when in training.

CAUTION
Use cook-off procedure only when in a combat environment.

3-6. PLANS AND PREPARATIONS FOR COMBAT

The theater commander normally establishes basic and combat loads of hand grenades. The combat load is not a fixed quantity; it can be altered as the situation dictates. Units vary their combat load depending upon the commander's analysis of METT-T. The most important factor in determining the combat load for hand grenades is unit mission. It influences the type and quantity of hand grenades needed. Other factors used in determining the hand grenade combat load are as follows:

a. **Weight**. Each hand grenade weighs close to one pound. Consequently, each grenade that the soldier carries adds another pound to his total load.

b. **Weapons Tradeoff**. Soldiers cannot carry everything commanders would like to take into battle. Commanders must consider the value of various weapons and munitions with a view toward determining which contribute the most to the mission accomplishment. For example, tradeoff may be required between hand grenades and mines, between hand grenades and mortar ammunition, or between different types of grenades.

c. **Balance**. Different types of hand grenades are required on all missions. Generally, fragmentation and colored smoke grenades are required for all missions. Distribute hand grenades selected for a mission among several soldiers, if not among all of them.

d. **Individual Duties**. Distribute to each soldier the hand grenades that are required for his job and assigned tasks.

3-7. EMPLOYMENT RULES

The rules to remember before employing hand grenades, or when in areas where they are in use, are as follows:

* Know where all friendly forces are located.
* Know your sector of fire.
* Use the buddy or team system.
* Ensure the projected arc of the fragmentation hand grenade is clear of obstacles.
* Evacuate positions into which you plan to throw a fragmentation hand grenade, if possible. If not, then use the grenade sump.

3-8. OFFENSIVE EMPLOYMENT

The fragmentation hand grenade is the primary type of grenade used during offensive operations. These grenades provide the violent, destructive, close-in firepower essential for the individual soldier to overcome and kill the enemy. The fragmentation hand grenade makes the individual soldier's movement easier by suppressing the enemy and disrupting the continuity of the enemy's defensive fires. Fragmentation hand grenades contribute greatly in destroying the enemy's will to continue the fight. The noise, flash, and concussion generated by fragmentation hand grenades have severe psychological effects on enemy soldiers. Offensive grenades are much less lethal than fragmentation grenades on an enemy in the open, but they are very effective against an enemy within a confined space. The concussion they produce is capable of killing or severely injuring enemy personnel, not just stunning them. Consider the following factors when employing hand grenades:

   a.   The critical phase of the attack is the final assault, that moment when a soldier closes with the enemy to kill him. The individual soldier uses the rifle, the hand grenade, and the bayonet during the assault. The soldier first uses the rifle, firing controlled, well-aimed shots at known or suspected enemy positions. The soldier does this as part of a buddy team, fire team, and squad. He is controlled and disciplined in his movement and application of fires by using the established unit SOPs and battle drills. These battle drills are rehearsed extensively during preparation for combat. As the soldier closes to hand grenade range, he engages the enemy with a combination of rifle fire and hand grenades. He uses fragmentation grenades to kill and suppress enemy soldiers in the open, in defilades, or in trenches. Movement toward the enemy is rapid and violent.

   b.   Soldiers must throw hand grenades accurately into enemy positions to reduce the chances of friendly hand grenades hitting friendly forces. Movement forward is done as part of a buddy team. One soldier within the buddy team provides overwatching, direct suppressive fire while the other soldier moves forward. Both soldiers must take advantage of the grenade explosion to immediately continue their movement forward. If the enemy is located in an enclosed area, such as a bunker or room within a building, the offensive grenade may be more appropriate than the fragmentation hand grenade. Choosing between them depends upon availability and mission analysis beforehand. Offensive grenades are less lethal to the enemy, but because of this, they are also safer to employ in confined spaces. Soldiers should follow offensive grenade employment immediately with violent rifle fire unless capturing enemy personnel is a mission requirement. Remember, an enemy who is only temporarily stunned can still kill you. The shock waves from an offensive grenade also provide better overall interior effect in an enclosed space. Another advantage of the offensive grenade is that it covers more of an enclosed space than the fragmentation grenade.

   c.   In an assault against a dug-in, well-prepared enemy, the soldier uses hand grenades to clear crew-served weapons first. Once the first defensive belt has been penetrated, he uses hand grenades in a priority effort to attack command bunkers and communications equipment and to kill or capture enemy leaders within those bunkers.

   d.   In the assault, the soldier participates as a squad member in clearing trenches, destroying bunkers, and clearing rooms. The soldier employs unit procedures, which have been rehearsed during preparation for combat. In clearing a trench within a fortified position (Figure 3-8), the buddy team forms the basis for all fragmentation grenade employment in the following manner:

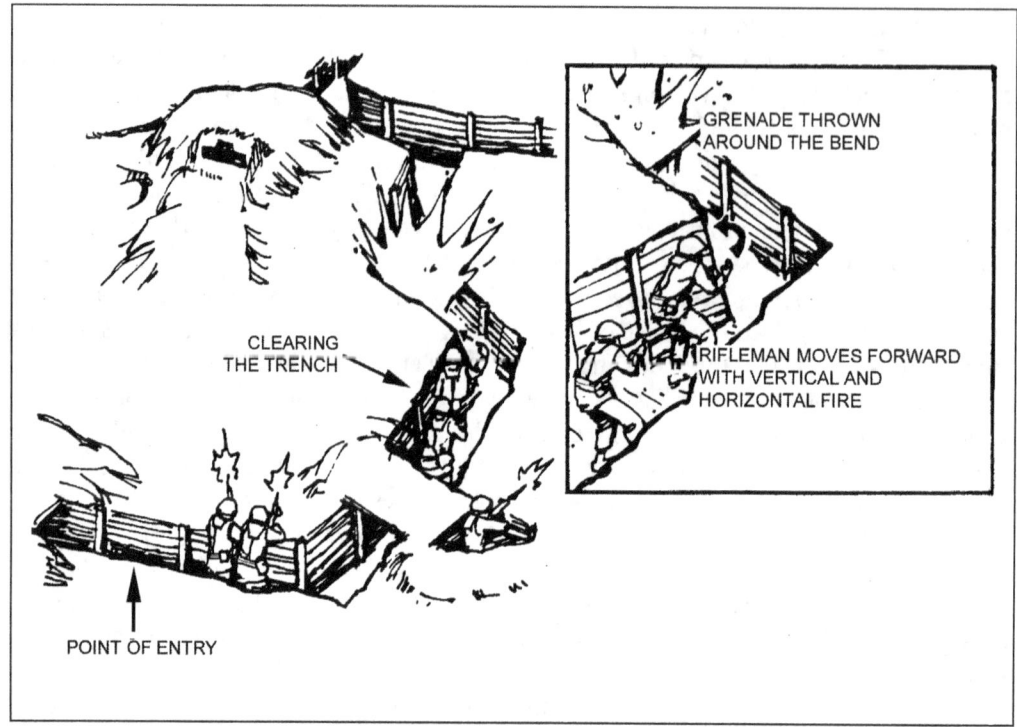

Figure 3-8. Enemy trench assault.

(1) Before entering the trench, the first clearing team throws or drops hand grenades into the trench, attempting to keep the individual grenades separated by at least five meters.

(2) After the grenades explode, the first clearing team rolls into the trench, landing on their feet and firing their weapons down both directions of the trench.

(3) The first clearing team holds the entry point.

(4) The teams following the first clearing team enter at the same position and begin clearing in one direction only (FM 7-8).

(5) As the lead buddy team moves to the right (or left), one soldier is the designated grenadier. He moves along the wall closest to the next bend in the trench. His movement is covered by his buddy, who is ready to fire at any enemy soldiers advancing toward them. The grenadier holds a grenade at the ready as he moves rapidly down the trench.

(6) At the bend in the trench, the designated grenadier throws a grenade around the bend. After the explosion, the rifleman moves rapidly around the bend and fires rapid bursts horizontally and alternately along the long axis of the trench.

(7) Movement down the trench continues by alternating the designated rifleman and grenadier roles or maintaining the same roles throughout. Fire teams and squads are bounded forward to continue clearing the trench line.

NOTE: The unit SOP specifies many of these tasks. If a three-man clearing team is used, the third member guards the back of the other team members and stands by to provide fire on point targets. (For action on the objective, see FM 7-8.)

e. Clearing an enemy bunker and killing the enemy soldiers inside requires violence and speed of execution, plus synchronization of effort at the buddy and squad level, in order to succeed. The following are procedures for clearing a bunker (Figure 3-9):

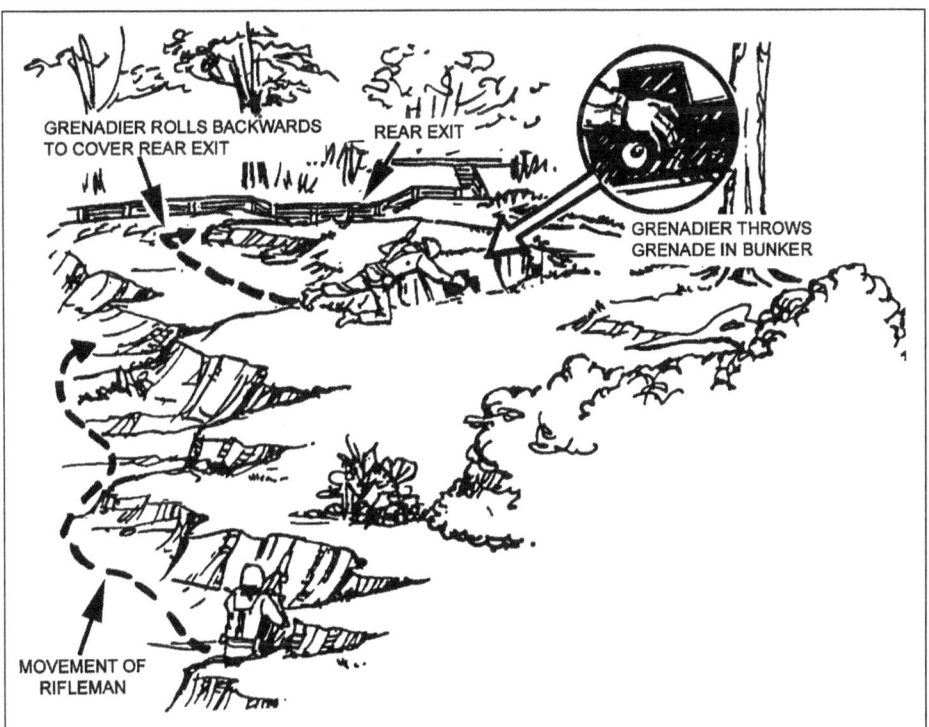

Figure 3-9. Enemy bunker assault.

(1) A two-man team assaults a single bunker using a combination of grenades and rifle fire. One member of the buddy team provides overwatching suppressive fire while the other member moves rapidly toward the bunker, using a combination of individual movement techniques. He uses the best available covered route to move toward the bunker.

(2) As he approaches to within 75 meters of the bunker, the grenadier can use white smoke to help conceal his movement for the remaining distance. The white smoke grenade should be thrown on line with the bunker and as close to the enemy's firing port as possible.

(3) Once the grenadier member of the buddy team is at the side of the bunker, he holds the grenade at a 90-degree angle from his body, releases the safety lever, mentally counts two seconds (ONE THOUSAND ONE, ONE THOUSAND TWO), and throws or pushes the grenade into the firing port of the bunker. Once he releases the grenade, he rolls away from the bunker and faces to the rear of the bunker, prepared to engage escaping enemy soldiers with his rifle.

(4) After the grenade detonates, he enters the position from the rear to kill or capture remaining enemy soldiers.

f. When clearing a room or moving through an urban area, the following considerations apply:

- What types of grenades do the ROE permit and restrict?
- What effect do I want to achieve--kill, stun, obscure, destroy equipment, mark a location, and so forth?
- Does the structural integrity of the room and building permit the types of grenades selected for use?
- Will the scheme of maneuver permit the use of fragmentation grenades and not cause fratricide?
- Will the type of grenade used cause an urban fire in an undesired location?

If employing grenades during room clearing, the following procedure should be used in conjunction with Battle Drill 6, FM 7-8, or Battle Drill 5, FM 7-7J:

(1) The Number 2 man throws a grenade into the room and yells FRAG OUT, STUN OUT, or CONCUSSION OUT, if stealth is not a factor, to alert friendly personnel that a grenade has been thrown toward the threat. After the grenade explodes, the Number 1 man enters the room, eliminates any threat, and moves to his point of domination IAW Battle Drill 6.

(2) Numbers 3 and 4 men enter the room, move to their points of domination, and eliminate any threat.

(3) The team clears and marks the room IAW unit SOP.

NOTE: Grenades tend to roll back down stairs and either nullify the desired effect(s) or cause friendly casualties.

g.   The use of hand grenades during raids always depends on the mission. The raid, as a type of offensive operation, is characterized by heavy use of fragmentation and offensive grenades, but it may also require other types of grenades. Use grenades according to the following guidelines:

(1) If the mission is to secure prisoners, the employment of offensive grenades is appropriate.

(2) If the mission calls for the destruction of vehicles, weapons, or special equipment, then incendiary grenades and fragmentation grenades are appropriate.

(3) Smoke grenades are often used to create a smoke screen covering the advance of friendly forces or to mark the location of friendly forces and pickup points. Colored smoke is used mainly for signaling purposes.

h.   Reaction to an enemy ambush requires an immediate, rapid, and violent response. The longer friendly forces remain in the ambush kill zone, the greater the probability of friendly force destruction. FM 7-8 and ARTEP 7-8 Drill describe friendly force reactions. Using a combination of fragmentation hand grenades to kill the enemy and white smoke grenades to obscure the enemy's sight and rifle fire, the soldiers within a squad assault the enemy force. Train and drill soldiers to throw fragmentation grenades first, then smoke grenades.

3-9.   DEFENSIVE EMPLOYMENT

Hand grenades are used in defensive operations during the final phase of the close-in battle. The primary hand grenade in all defensive operations is the fragmentation grenade. It is used in conjunction with other weapons and man-made or natural obstacles to destroy remnants of the attacking enemy force that have succeeded in penetrating the more distant barriers and final protective fires. The fragmentation hand grenade further disrupts the continuity of the enemy attack, demoralizes the enemy soldier, and forces the enemy into areas covered by direct-fire weapons, such as rifle and machine gun fire and Claymore mines. Using fragmentation hand grenades on dismounted enemy forces at a critical moment in the assault can be the final blow in taking the initiative away from the enemy.

a. **Defense From Individual Fighting Positions** (Figure 3-10). From individual fighting positions, fragmentation hand grenades are used primarily to cover close-in dead space approaches on the friendly side of the protective wire and in front of a squad's position. Soldiers should use these grenades in conjunction with ground flares positioned along the protective wire. Enemy soldiers who are stopped at the protective wire are engaged first with Claymore mines. If time permits during the preparation of the defensive position, soldiers should identify dead space in their sectors, especially dead space that may intersect the protective wire and move toward the friendly fighting positions. These potential avenues of approach through the protective wire should be marked with a reference to identify them as primary hand grenade targets. The following rules apply when employing fragmentation hand grenades from fighting positions:

(1) Clear overhead obstructions that may interfere with the path of the thrown grenade. Do this at the same time direct-fire fields of fire are cleared.

(2) Rehearse grenade employment; know where your primary target is located.

(3) Keep 50 percent of your fragmentation grenades at the ready in your fighting position, leaving the remaining fragmentation grenades on your load-carrying equipment (LCE).

(4) Rehearse actions needed if an enemy grenade lands in your fighting position.

(5) Employ fragmentation hand grenades against enemy soldiers located in defilade positions as first priority. This lessens the danger to friendly soldiers and helps cover terrain not covered by direct-fire weapons. Use the rifle to kill enemy soldiers not in defilade positions.

(6) Reconnoiter the alternate and supplementary positions and determine the priority for the fragmentation hand grenade target.

(7) Redistribute hand grenades after each enemy engagement.

WARNING
Former Soviet Union grenades use fuzes with only a 3- to 4-second delay, which means you have very little time to react. The preferred course of action if an enemy grenade lands in your position or near you is to immediately roll out of your fighting position or throw yourself flat on the ground.

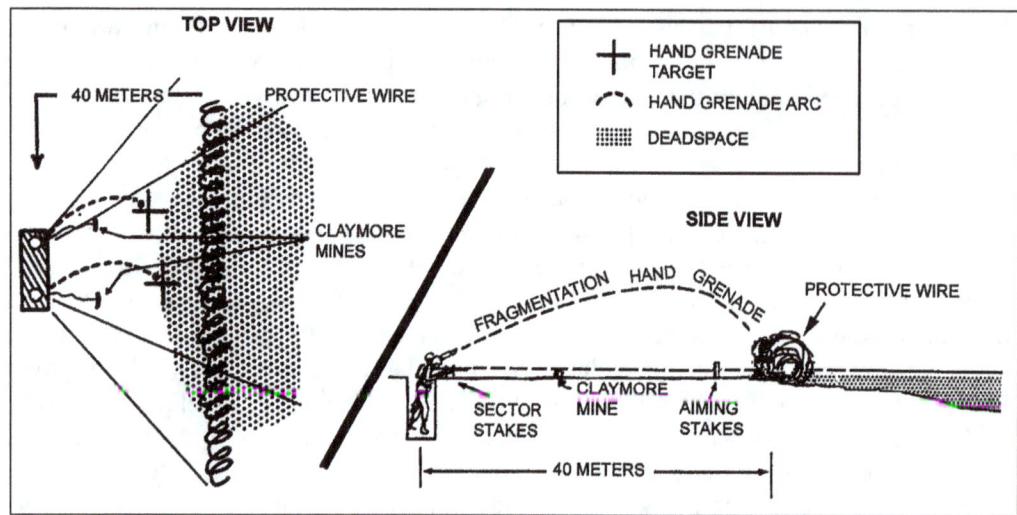

Figure 3-10. Defense from an individual fighting position.

b. **Defense Against Enemy Armored and Tracked Vehicles** (Figure 3-11). On occasion, friendly dismounted soldiers may come in close contact with enemy armored formations. Dismounted infantry should first use antitank weapons to defeat enemy armor and motorized infantry. Soldiers can also use satchel charges, as described in FM 5-250, to defeat enemy armor. If these are not available, it is still possible to destroy, immobilize, or render inoperative the vehicle or system, or to kill the crew inside the vehicle. In either case, the soldier must approach the armored vehicle to kill it or the crew with hand grenades. An understanding of some characteristics and vulnerabilities of former Soviet Union armor can help kill or disable the enemy armored vehicle or its crew. Vulnerabilities common to most threat vehicles are the fuel cells, ammunition storage areas, and power trains. Figure 3-12 highlights vulnerable areas on selected threat vehicles.

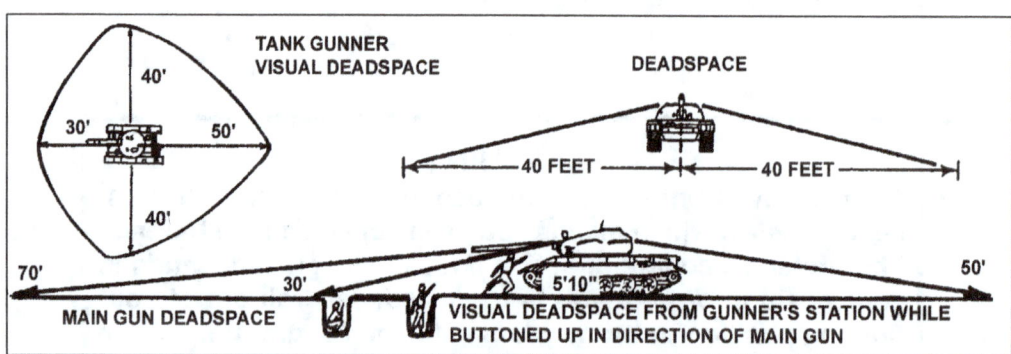

Figure 3-11. Attack of a former Soviet Union tank.

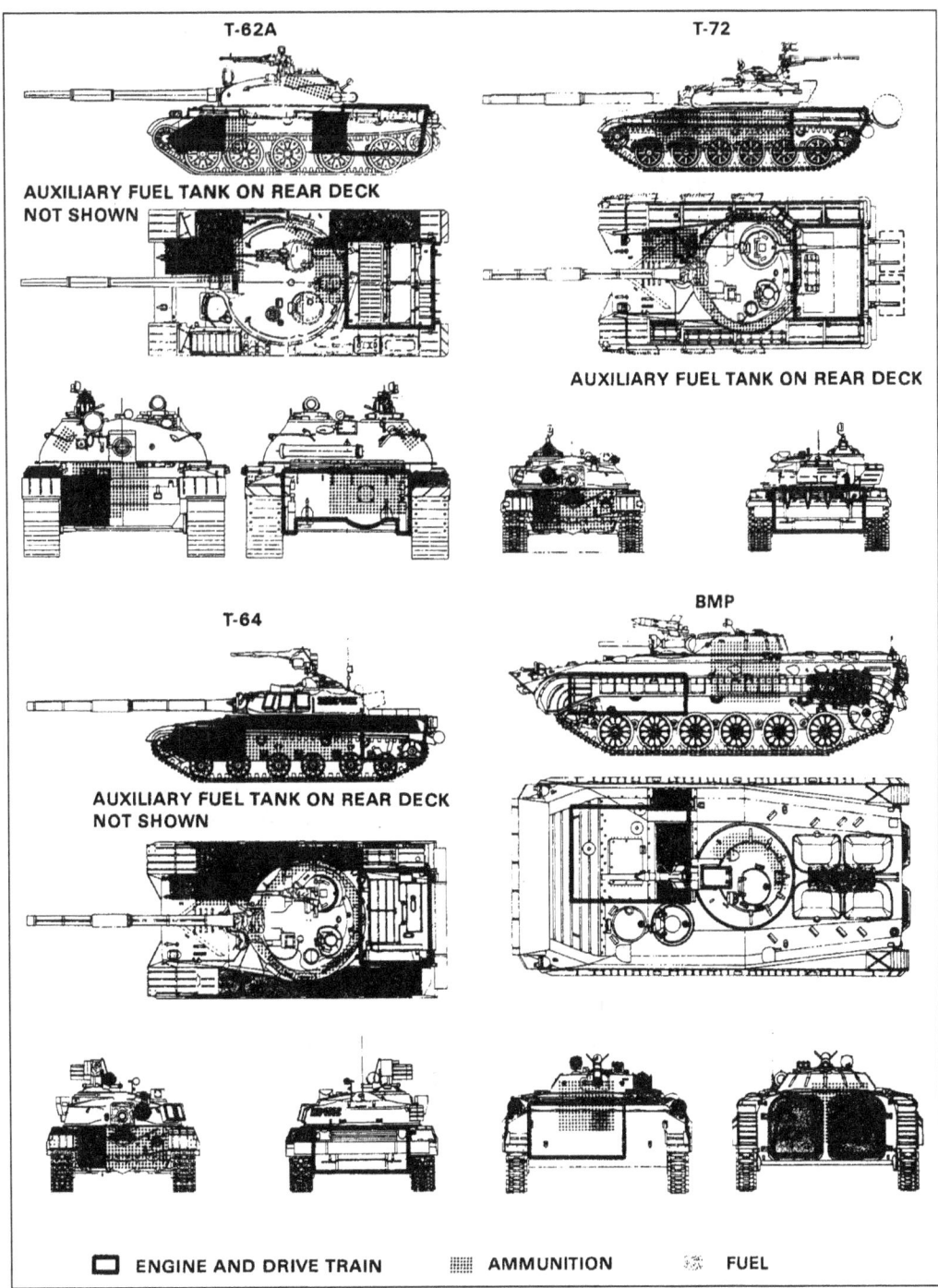

Figure 3-12. Former Soviet Union vehicle vulnerabilities.

(1) *Turret rotation*. The turrets of older former Soviet Union tanks rotate much slower than those on US and NATO tanks. It takes more than 21 seconds for T60- and T70-series tanks to rotate through a full 360 degrees. The T80- and T90-series (Figure 3-13) tanks rotate a full 360 degrees in just 6 seconds, which is as fast as the US's M1 Abrams and M2 BFV. With the older former Soviet Union tanks, a soldier can actually run around the tank before the turret traverses from the front deck to the rear. The newer tanks have been fitted with explosive reactive armor, which makes them more difficult to engage with antitank weapons. Therefore, engagement with hand grenades should be considered only as a last resort.

(2) *Visual dead space*. From the gunner's station of a former Soviet Union tank, nothing at ground level within 30 feet can be seen through the frontal 180 degrees of turret rotation. If the turret is oriented over the rear 180 degrees (the rear deck), the dead space increases to 50 feet. This means gunners on former Soviet Union tanks cannot see soldiers in fighting positions within these distances of the tank.

(3) *Fire extinguisher system*. A fire extinguisher system can be triggered manually or automatically by one of eight heat sensors. The fire extinguisher's ethylene bromide gas creates a poisonous vapor when exposed to flames. If the extinguisher discharges, the crew may have to bail out. Any weapon that can trigger a fire and the fire extinguisher system might possibly knock out a former Soviet Union tank.

(4) *BMP visual dead space*. The BMP has nine vision blocks for the eight infantrymen in the rear of the vehicle. Eight of these vision blocks, four on each side, correspond to the firing ports for the squad's weapons. These vision blocks are oriented at a 45-degree angle toward the vehicle's direction of movement. The soldier at the left rear of the vehicle mans either the left rear vision block or the last vision block and firing port on the left side. If the flank firing port is being manned, the vehicle is vulnerable to an approach from the rear. Dismounted soldiers should attempt to destroy or disable enemy armor only as a last resort. When employing hand grenades for this purpose, follow these procedures:

- Remain in a covered fighting position until the vehicle closes to within its visual dead space. Approach the vehicle from the rear, moving aggressively.
- Place an incendiary grenade over the engine compartment.
- Attempt to drop a fragmentation grenade into an open hatch if incendiary grenades are not available.
- Engage any crewmen who exit the vehicle.

c. **Defensive Employment on Urban Terrain**. The considerations for the defensive employment of grenades on urban terrain are generally the same as offensive considerations with respect to ROE, structural integrity of the building, fratricide avoidance, and desired effects of the type grenade to be used. Additionally, the following also apply:

(1) Fragmentation grenades can be very effective in producing casualties when thrown at assaulting enemy troops between buildings or on streets from windows, doors, mouseholes, or other building apertures.

(2) Stun grenades can cause confusion and hesitation when thrown at assaulting enemy soldiers, allowing time for withdrawal from rooms. This is especially useful if the structural integrity of the building does not permit the use of fragmentation or concussion grenades.

(3) Use of smoke grenades inside buildings may displace oxygen in poorly ventilated rooms and make breathing difficult while also rendering protective masks ineffective.

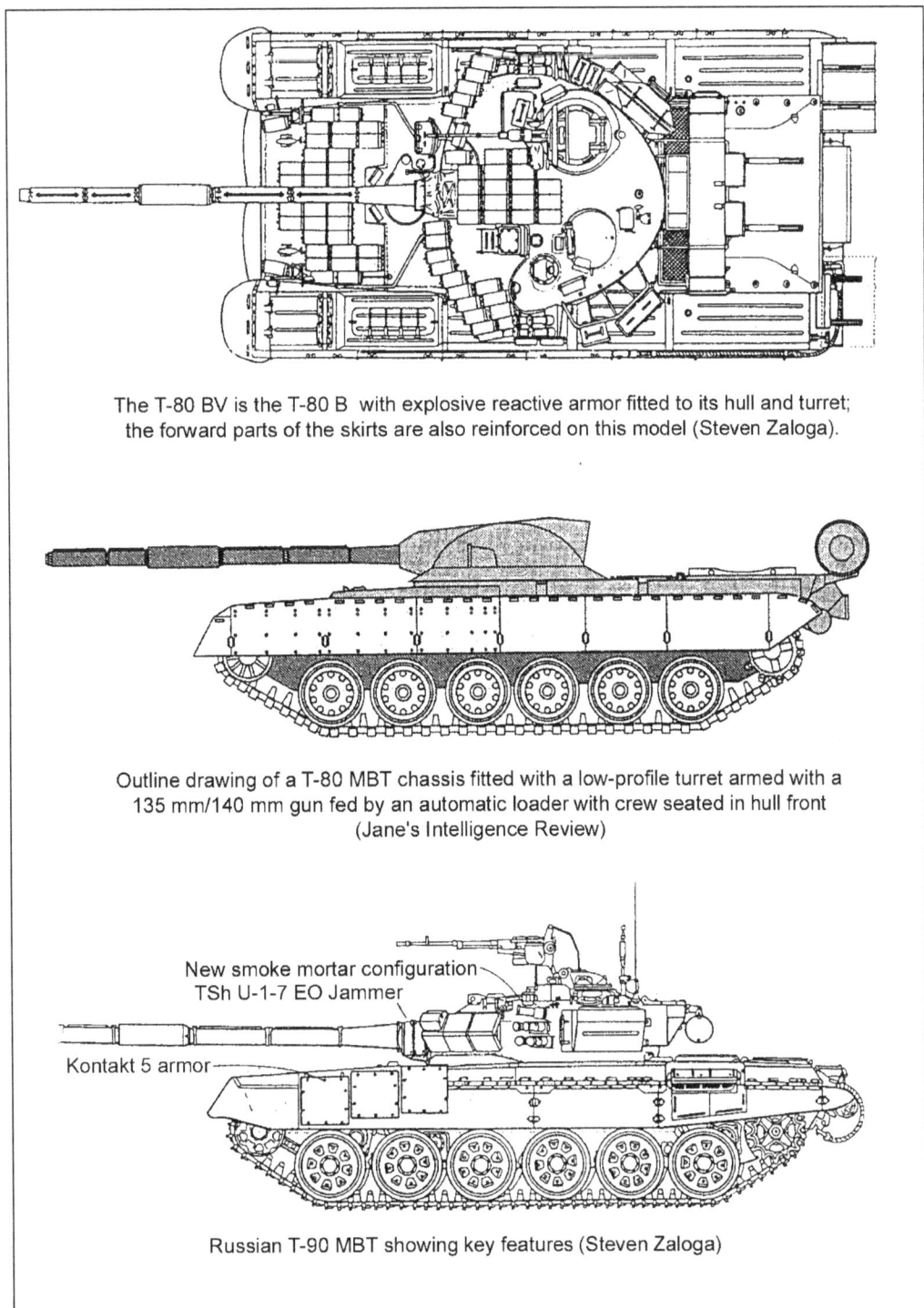

The T-80 BV is the T-80 B with explosive reactive armor fitted to its hull and turret; the forward parts of the skirts are also reinforced on this model (Steven Zaloga).

Outline drawing of a T-80 MBT chassis fitted with a low-profile turret armed with a 135 mm/140 mm gun fed by an automatic loader with crew seated in hull front (Jane's Intelligence Review)

New smoke mortar configuration
TSh U-1-7 EO Jammer

Kontakt 5 armor

Russian T-90 MBT showing key features (Steven Zaloga)

Figure 3-13. T80- and T90-series former Soviet Union tanks.

3-10. RETROGRADE OPERATIONS EMPLOYMENT

Most of the employment considerations applicable to the use of hand grenades in the defense are equally applicable to retrograde operations. Special applications or considerations for hand grenade use during retrograde operations relate to creating obstacles, marking friendly force locations, and breaking contact.

a. **Create Obstacles**. When terrain conditions permit, soldiers can use incendiary grenades to impede and disrupt enemy movement by initiating fires in specific areas.

b. **Mark Locations**. Soldiers can use colored smoke hand grenades to mark friendly force positions and identify friendly forces.

c. **Break Contact**. During retrograde operations, some elements of the friendly force most often become decisively engaged. Soldiers can use fragmentation, white smoke, and CS grenades to break contact and regain flexibility of maneuver. Use of hand grenades in volley fire following the employment of white smoke is especially effective. The smoke obscures enemy observation of friendly force movement from covered positions, and the fragmentation grenades force the enemy to cover.

3-11. REAR AREA OPERATIONS EMPLOYMENT

Army operations doctrine recognizes that the nature of a future war poses a significant threat to rear areas. These threats range from large operational maneuver groups to highly trained, special operating forces and even terrorists. All US soldiers in combat, CS, and CSS units must be prepared to fight using small arms, antitank weapons, Claymore mines, and fragmentation grenades. At every element level throughout the corps battle area, individual US soldiers must react to every action by aggressive, violent employment of grenades and individual weapons. There is no safe zone on the battlefield; therefore, leaders must plan for the following:

a. **Special Considerations**. Two features of rear area operations provide for unique considerations concerning hand grenade employment. In certain areas of the world, the US Army and its allies must anticipate a large number of civilian refugees moving into and through the rear area. This situation can be confusing with the large numbers of CS and CSS units operating throughout the rear area. These factors dictate the following guidelines for hand grenade employment in the rear areas:

(1) *Offensive grenades*. Individual soldiers throw offensive grenades at enemy soldiers in situations where noncombatants and support troops may be intermingled with threat forces.

(2) *Riot-control grenades*. It is reasonable to expect enemy special forces, special agent provocateurs, and fifth columnists to attempt to incite riots in our rear areas, especially if the conflict begins to stalemate and does not result in the rapid victory for either side. Forces in the rear area must quell these riots as rapidly as possible while reducing damage to the lives and property of noncombatants. Riot-control grenades, which are usually associated with peacetime law and order functions, also have relevancy in maintaining control of the rear area.

b. **Base Cluster Defense**. Base cluster commanders must organize the defense of their positions in much the same manner as tactical commanders in the MBA. Accordingly, the employment of hand grenades from defense positions surrounding the base cluster should follow the same considerations as hand grenade employment by combat units in the MBA.

3-12. USE UNDER ADVERSE CONDITIONS

While hand grenade procedures do not change when employed under adverse conditions, special cautions must be considered.

a. **MOPP4**. Exercise additional caution when employing hand grenades in MOPP gear. The thrower should execute arming and throwing procedures carefully and deliberately and should concentrate on using the proper grip. Observing each arming action (removal of safety clip and safety pin) is also recommended in MOPP. Note that wearing gloves inhibits the thrower's feel and could decrease his throwing ability and range.

b. **Night**. Throwers must have clear fields of fire with no overhead obstructions. Depth perception is generally impaired under limited visibility conditions.

CHAPTER 4

TRAINING PROGRAM

The intended outcome of all hand grenade training programs is to train soldiers proficient in using hand grenades for any tactical situation. The training program should incorporate safe handling and throwing practices, which reduce injuries in peacetime as well as in combat. Initially, training programs require extensive direct supervision, but the amount of supervision required decreases as the soldiers' proficiency increases.

4-1. OBJECTIVES

The hand grenade training program progresses using the crawl-walk-run methodology. The program progresses from fundamental to advanced training, culminating with the integration of hand grenades into situational and field training exercises. Once soldiers reach a high-proficiency level, a sustainment program is implemented to maintain this level. The following progressive training outline is for use or modification:

- Instruction on safety inspection and maintenance of hand grenades.
- Instruction on visual identification of hand grenades.
- Instruction on capabilities of hand grenades.
- Technical instruction on grenade function.
- Instruction and practical exercises on fundamentals of gripping procedures, throwing techniques, and throwing positions.
- Practical exercises emphasizing distance and accuracy using targets of different types at various ranges.
- Advanced training courses that incorporate buddy teams, movement techniques, weapon integration, and multiple target engagements at various ranges.

4-2. TRAINING COURSES

The training courses listed in this chapter, except for the standard Army hand grenade qualification course, are offered as models to assist units in meeting their training objectives. These courses can be modified to support the unit METL, the terrain, and the commander's intent. Minimum course standards for basic training units have training stations that include the following:

a. **Distance and Accuracy**. The distance and accuracy course is designed to develop the soldier's proficiency in gripping and throwing hand grenades. When conducting the training, provide soldiers with a course orientation, explanation, and demonstration, including clarification of the tasks, conditions, and standards for the course and followed by a demonstration that meets the stated standards. To develop good safety habits, supervisors and instructors must ensure the soldiers use proper throwing techniques. During the initial practical exercise, soldiers are allowed to observe the strike of the grenade so they can gain an appreciation for the weight of the grenade and the amount of force required to throw it accurately. After initial training, however, soldiers should follow the proper procedures for seeking cover after throwing a grenade. The following is a generic task with conditions and standards to assist units.

TASK: Engage a variety of targets at varying ranges up to 40 meters.

CONDITIONS: Given 12 practice grenades, individual equipment, and a four-station course with a variety of targets at distances of 20, 30, and 40 meters.

STANDARDS: The soldier must successfully engage targets at each station with two out of three grenades. The soldier must throw from the alternate prone, prone to kneeling, and prone to standing positions. A target is successfully engaged when the grenade detonates within 5 meters of the target.

(1) Recommend a four-station course layout (Figure 4-1). The four stations may be combined if the terrain does not allow four stations.

(2) Targets should include soldiers in the open at 20 meters, a fortified mortar pit at 20 meters, a fighting position at 30 meters, and a trench target at 40 meters.

b. **Bunker Complex**. The bunker complex (Figure 3-9, page 3-13) exercise is designed to develop the soldier's proficiency on how to properly attack a bunker complex from a covered and concealed location while using the proper movement techniques and the hand grenade cook-off technique. When conducting the training, give soldiers clarification on the task, conditions, and standards, followed by a demonstration and standards for the station. The following is a generic task with conditions and standards to assist units.

TASK: Engage an enemy bunker complex.

CONDITIONS: Given an individual weapon, LCE, cover and concealment, supportive fire, and two M69 practice hand grenades.

STANDARDS: The soldier must successfully engage and disable a bunker. The soldier must approach the bunker from the blind side, properly cook-off the grenade, put the grenade into the porthole of the bunker, roll away from the bunker, and turn 180 degrees to cover the rear exit of the bunker. The grenade must detonate in the bunker.

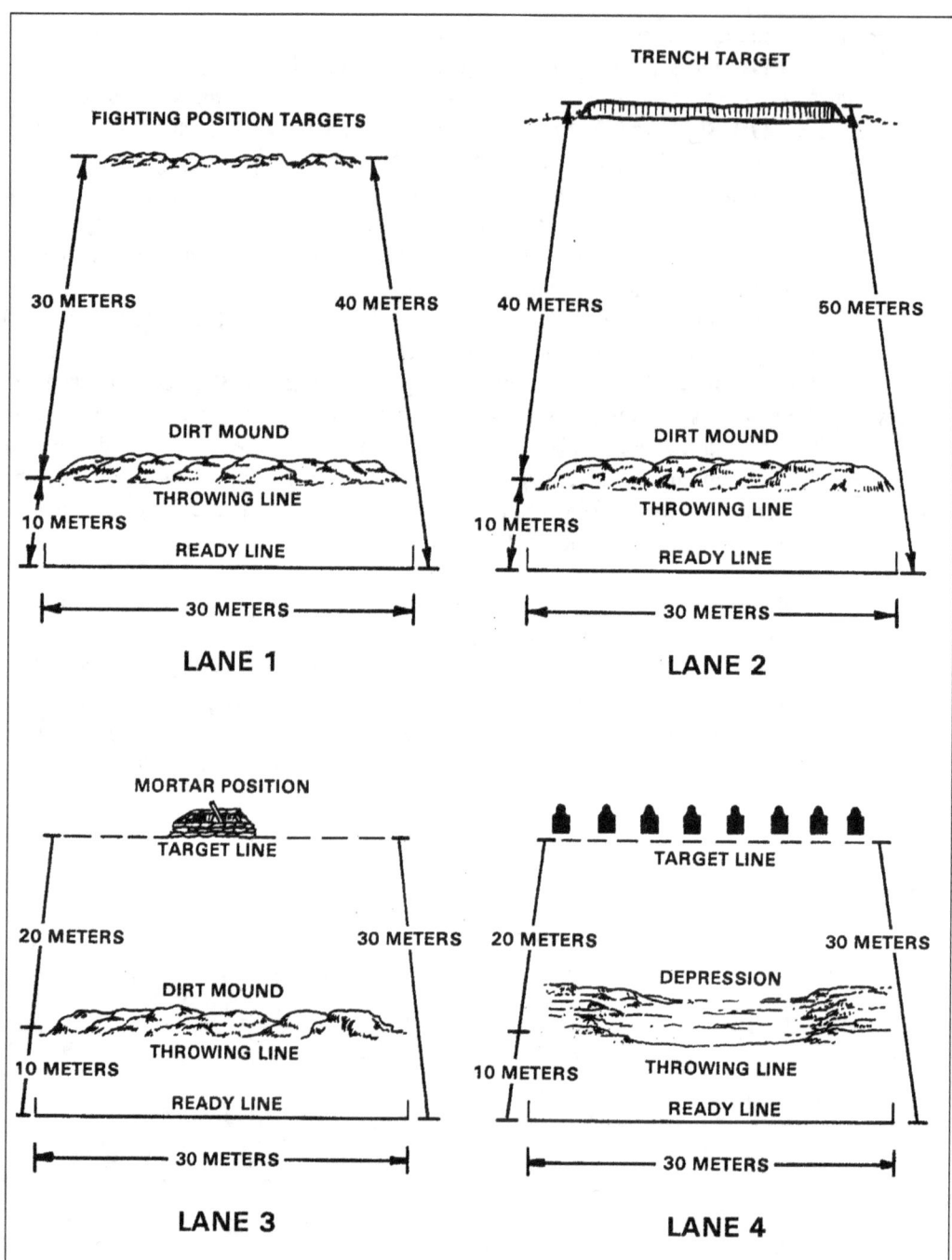

Figure 4-1. Distance and accuracy layout.

c. **Identification of Basic US Army Hand Grenades**. The purpose of this training is to develop the soldier's proficiency in identifying basic hand grenades within the US Army inventory. The soldier should receive instruction on the capabilities and identification features of the M83, M18, M14, ABC-M7A2/A3, and the M67 fragmentation hand grenades. For seasoned soldiers, other hand grenades can be added for test purposes to increase the soldiers' ability to identify other grenades. Basic training recruits must identify five out of five grenades in order to get a GO.

d. **Hand Grenade Qualification Course**. The purpose of the qualification course is to measure and evaluate the soldier's ability to engage a variety of targets with hand grenades using the proper gripping procedures and throwing techniques. The qualification course allows the soldier to gain confidence in arming and throwing hand grenades. All soldiers must go through mock-bay training before going to live bay. The qualification course should not be attempted until all initial training has been completed. The qualification course allows soldiers to use fuzed practice hand grenades to engage targets in natural terrain under simulated combat conditions. An incentive for a soldier to perform well is the award of a hand grenade qualification bar worn on his marksmanship medal. The hand grenade qualification course is standardized throughout the US Army. The course consists of seven stations with one grader at each station. The course is conducted in two-man teams, but soldiers are evaluated individually. The stations' requirements are as follows:

- Station 1. Engage a group of F-type silhouette targets in the open from a two-man fighting position. The targets are located 35 meters to the front of the fighting position, simulating enemy movement through and beyond the squad's protective wire.

- Station 2. Engage a bunker using available cover and concealment. The bunker can have one or two firing portholes oriented toward the direction of the buddy team's movement and a rear exit.

- Station 3. Engage a fortified 82-mm mortar position from 20 meters.

- Station 4. Engage a group of enemy targets behind cover at a 20-meter distance.

- Station 5. Clear an entry point to a trench line at a 25-meter distance.

- Station 6. Engage troops in a halted, open-type wheeled vehicle at a 25-meter distance.

- Station 7. Identify hand grenades. Soldiers must be able to identify grenades by shape, color, markings, and capabilities. (For a suggested identification station, refer to Figure 4-2.)

Although no two hand grenade qualification courses are alike, the standards must be consistent. The scorecard at Figures 4-3 (front) and 4-4 (back) establishes the action, condition, standard, and scoring procedure for the qualification course. DA Form 3517-R is located in Appendix G of this manual and can be locally reproduced on 8 1/2- by 11-inch paper. Qualification must be awarded only to those soldiers who meet these standards. The evaluator at each station determines scoring IAW the standard scorecard. (For an example of a physical layout, see Figure 4-5.)

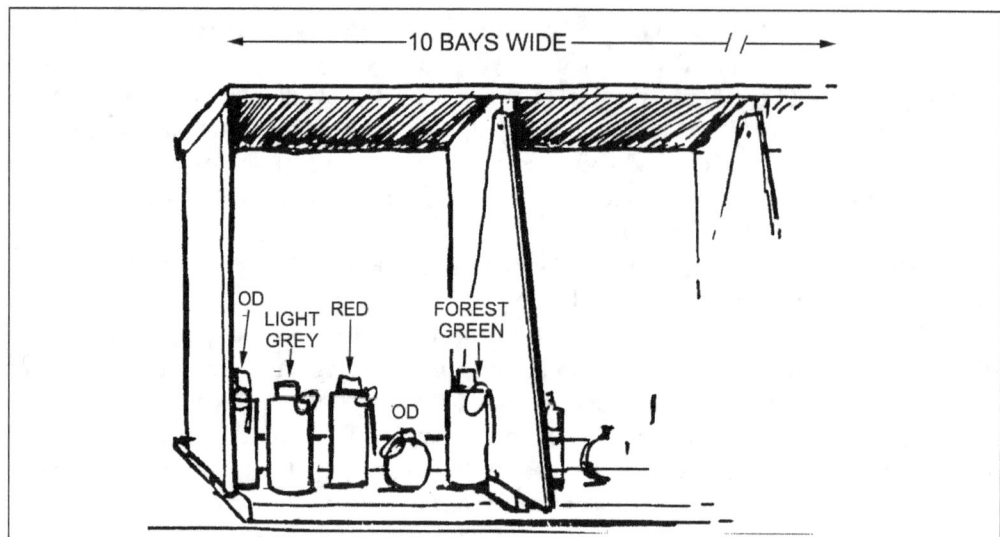

Figure 4-2. Suggested identification station.

HAND GRENADE QUALIFICATION SCORECARD
For use of this form, see FM 23-30. The proponent agency is TRADOC.

NOTE: In addition to the requirements on this scorecard, the soldier must throw two live fragmentation grenades to qualify.

A. DATE LIVE GRENADES WERE THROWN	B. INITIALS
6 March 2000	CAM

C. NAME (Last, First, Middle Initial)	D. DATE
Martinez, Carlos A.	6 March 2000

E. GRADE	F. SSN	G. UNIT
E7	123-45-6789	A Co, 2/29

H. STATION	I. TYPE TARGET	J. GO	K. NO-GO	L. SCORER'S INITIALS
1	Engage Enemy from Fighting Position at a Range of 35 Meters (Standing)	✓		S.T.
2	Engage Bunker	✓		K.F.
3	Engage 82-mm Mortar Position at 20 Meters (Kneeling)	✓		L.J.
4	Engage Enemy Behind Cover at 20 Meters (Alternate Prone)	✓		J.P.
5	Engage Trench at 25 Meters (Standing)	✓		J.C.
6	Engage Wheeled Vehicle at 25 Meters (Kneeling)		✓	M.S.
7	Identify Hand Grenades	✓		D.F.

M. QUALIFICATION STANDARD		CHECK
PASSED 7	EXPERT	
PASSED 6	FIRST CLASS	✓
PASSED 5	SECOND CLASS	
PASSED 4 OR LESS	UNQUALIFIED	

N. SIGNATURE OF SCORER/OIC

E. R. Stone

DA FORM 3517-R ___ 99   DA FORM 3517-R, NOV 88, IS OBSOLETE.

Figure 4-3. Example of a scorecard (front).

STATION 1. Engage Enemy from Fighting Position at a Range of 35 Meters *(Standing)*			STATION 5. Engage Trench at 25 Meters *(Standing)*		
PERFORMANCE MEASURES	GO	NO-GO	PERFORMANCE MEASURES	GO	NO-GO
A. Detonated at least one grenade within 5 meters of the center of target.	✓		A. Detonated at least one grenade inside trench.	✓	
B. Kept exposure time under 3 seconds.	✓		B. Kept exposure time under 3 seconds.	✓	
C. Returned to covered position after each throw.	✓		C. Returned to covered position after each throw.	✓	
D. Used proper grip.	✓		D. Used proper grip.	✓	
E. Used proper throwing techniques.	✓		E. Used proper throwing techniques.	✓	
F. Completed performance measures 1A through 1E within 15 seconds.	✓		STATION 6. Engage Wheeled Vehicle at 25 Meters *(Kneeling)*		
STATION 2. Engage Bunker			A. Detonated within 1 meter of vehicle or within 5 meters of dismounting troops.	✓	
A. Approached from blind side.	✓		B. Kept exposure time under 3 seconds.	✓	
B. Checked for bunker opening.	✓		C. Returned to covered position after each throw.	✓	
C. Detonated grenade in bunker.	✓		D. Used proper grip.		✓
D. Rolled away from bunker.	✓		E. Used proper throwing techniques.	✓	
E. Used proper grip.	✓		F. Completed performance measures 6A through 6E within 15 seconds.	✓	
F. Use cook-off technique.	✓		STATION 7. Identify Hand Grenades		
G. Completed performance measures 2A through 2E within 15 seconds.	✓		A. Selected fragmentation grenade to engage enemy soldiers.	✓	
STATION 3. Engage 82-mm Mortar Position at 20 Meters *(Kneeling)*			B. Identified M83 grenade as "White Smoke" or "HC smoke."	✓	
A. Detonated at least one grenade inside mortar position.	✓		C. Identified M18 grenade as "Colored Smoke" or "Purple (and so forth) Smoke." *(If specific color is stated, it must be the same color as on the training aid grenade used.)*	✓	
B. Kept exposure time under 3 seconds.	✓				
C. Returned to covered position after each throw.	✓		D. Identified M7A2/A3 grenade as CS or riot control.	✓	
D. Used proper grip.	✓		E. Identified M14 grenades as incendiary.	✓	
E. Used proper throwing techniques.	✓				
F. Completed performance measures 3A through 3E within 15 seconds.	✓		NOTES: 1. FOR PERFORMANCE MEASURES 7A THROUGH 7E, IF THE EXAMINEE CANNOT CORRECTLY STATE THE NAME OF THE GRENADE BUT CAN CORRECTLY IDENTIFY ITS USE, THEN THE EXAMINEE IS SCORED A "GO."		
STATION 4. Engage Enemy Behind Cover at 20 Meters *(Alternate Prone)*					
A. Detonated at least one grenade within 5 meters of the center of target.	✓		2. EACH PERFORMANCE MEASURE AT EACH SECTION IS GRADED ON A PASS/FAIL STANDARD. A SOLDIER MUST PASS ALL OF THE STANDARDS TO RECEIVE A "GO" ON THAT STATION.		
B. Kept exposure time under 3 seconds.	✓				
C. Returned to covered position after each throw.	✓				
D. Used proper grip.	✓				
E. Used proper throwing techniques.	✓				
F. Completed performance measures 4A through 4E within 15 seconds.	✓				

REVERSE OF DA FORM 3517-R, ___ 99

Figure 4-4. Example of a scorecard (back).

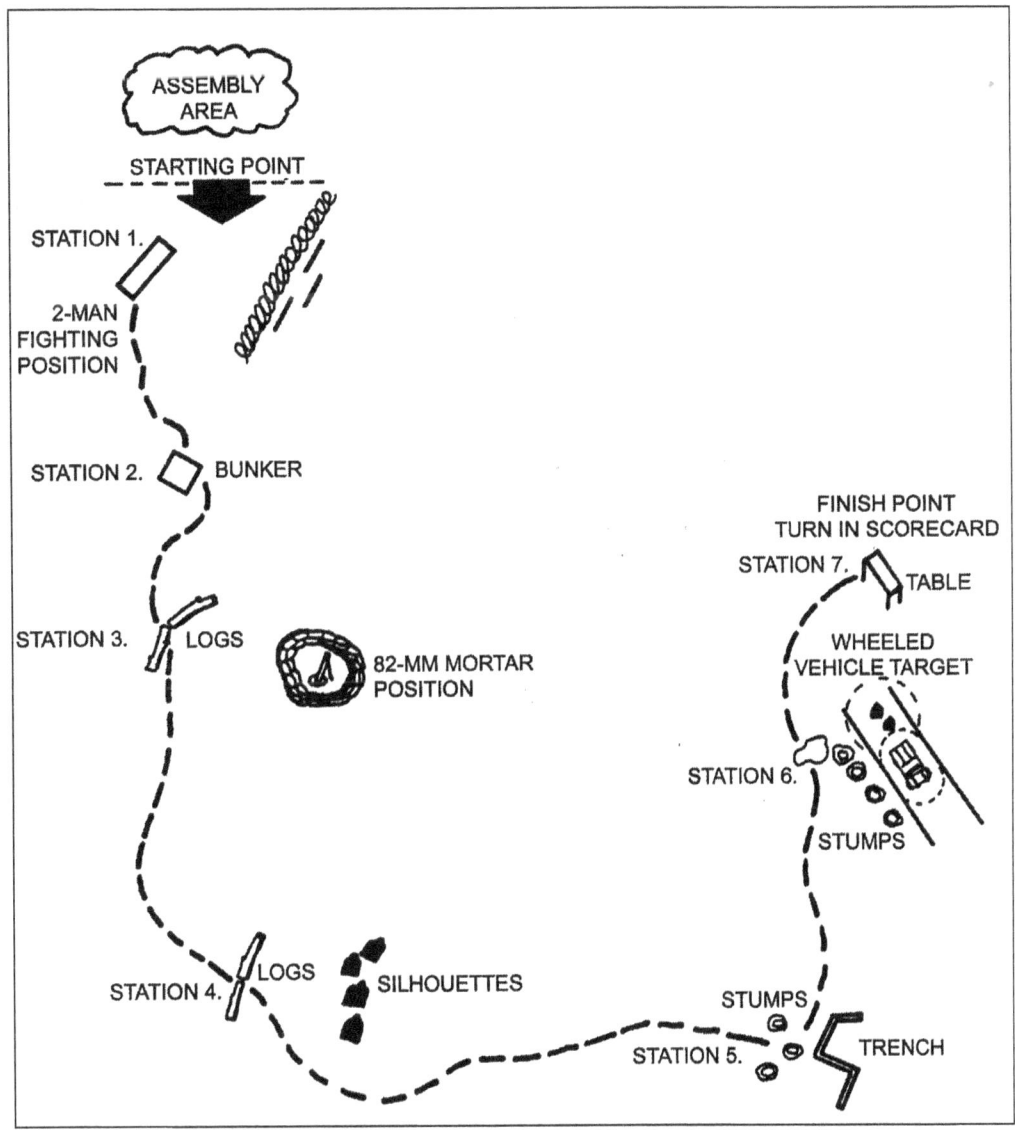

Figure 4-5. Qualification course layout.

e. **Mock-Bay Training**. When soldiers practice throwing grenades before going to live bay to throw, it is called mock-bay training. This training introduces the soldier to throwing commands and provides additional throwing practice. Soldiers are oriented to the mock-bay training pit and given an explanation of the commands that are used during actual throwing. Soldiers also practice the actual procedures used during live-bay training. The instructor enforces correct throwing and safety procedures. Improper techniques or bad habits, which a soldier could carry over to live-bay training, cannot be tolerated. The following is a generic task with conditions and standards to assist units:

TASK: Successfully throw practice hand grenades from the mock-bay pit and follow all commands from the instructor or NCOIC.

CONDITIONS: Given individual equipment, to include flak vest, practice hand grenades, a mock-bay pit that replicates a live-bay pit, ear plugs, and an orientation and safety briefing.

STANDARDS: Soldiers must safely carry, arm, and throw two practice hand grenades from the mock-bay pit while following the commands from the instructor or NCOIC. Soldiers must not move from the cover of the pit until the command CLEAR, ALL CLEAR is given.

NOTE: Be sure the physical layout of the mock-bay pit replicates the live-bay pit. This technique not only gives the soldier the sensation of throwing a live fragmentation hand grenade, but also instills confidence in his ability to throw the hand grenade and shows him its lethality. The procedures and techniques for conducting live hand grenade range operations depend upon available facilities and their regulations. Each facility has its own safety features and training qualities, so it is difficult to standardize the operating procedures.

f. **Live-Bay Training**. The purpose of the live-bay pit is to give soldiers the opportunity to experience throwing a live fragmentation hand grenade. The following guidelines are provided to assist in the conduct of live hand grenade training:

(1) Soldiers must have mock-bay training before throwing live grenades at live bay.

(2) Soldiers must receive a safety briefing before throwing live grenades.

(3) Throughout hand grenade training, especially at a live-bay pit, instructors must instill confidence in the soldiers, not apprehension. Hand grenades are inherently safe when used properly.

(4) Soldiers throwing live hand grenades must have a target. This makes sense tactically and provides a safer training environment. Consult the local range regulations for any restrictions.

(5) If facilities permit, an observation window allows the soldiers to observe the live-bay throwing procedures before and after throwing the hand grenades. (For a suggested live-bay layout, see Figures 4-6 and 4-7.)

(6) Soldiers must carry the hand grenades to the throwing pits using the proper right or left handgrips.

(7) Soldiers must wear flak vests, Kevlars, ear plugs, and eye armor, if available.

NOTE: Instructors check the soldiers using the Live Hand Grenade Range Operations Checklist in Appendix A.

Figure 4-6. Live-bay throwing pit.

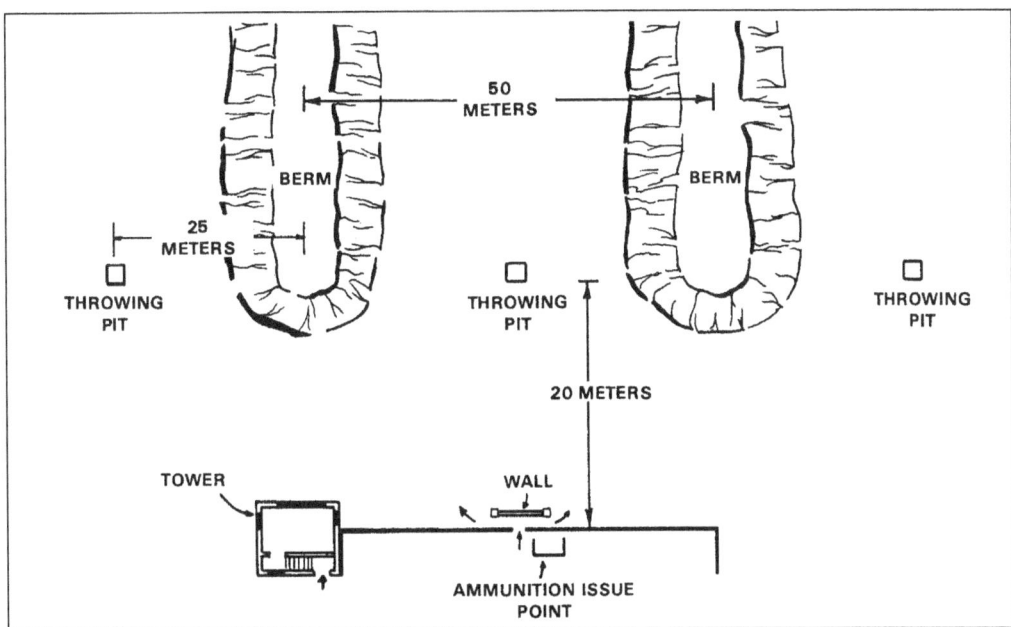

Figure 4-7. Suggested live-bay layout.

The following is a generic task with conditions and standards to assist units.

    TASK: Engage targets with live fragmentation grenades.

    CONDITIONS: Given individual equipment, to include Kevlar, LCE, flak vest, earplugs, a facility for live hand grenade throwing, and live fragmentation hand grenades.

STANDARDS: The soldier must safely arm and throw two live fragmentation hand grenades. The soldier must carry grenades using the proper right or left handgrips and comply with all throwing commands and instructions from the pit NCO.

g. **Hand Grenade Confidence Course**. Once the soldier has developed his throwing proficiency and has been introduced to throwing casualty-producing hand grenades, he needs an opportunity to apply his newly acquired proficiency in a simulated tactical situation requiring the use of grenades. The hand grenade confidence course is designed to accomplish this objective (Figure 4-8). The hand grenade confidence course has a practice and live course, each consisting of an assembly area, a final coordination line, an initial holding area, a covering position, a throwing position, and a final holding area. The following guidance is given to initiate the confidence course:

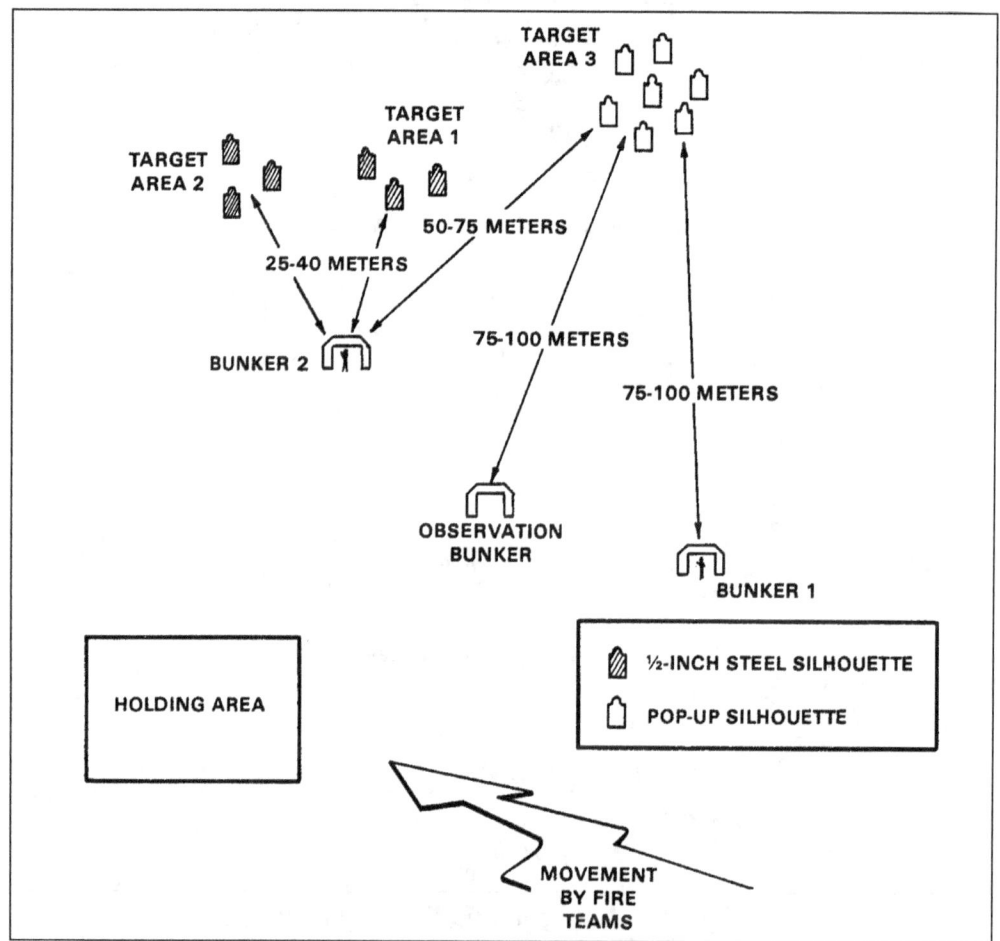

Figure 4-8. Confidence course layout.

(1) *Conduct of course.*

(a) The course begins with an orientation period covering the characteristics and functioning of practice and fragmentation hand grenades, safety considerations governing the conduct of training, and a discussion and demonstration of the conduct of the course for the entire unit being trained.

(b) Following the initial orientation, each platoon moves to a separate assembly area for the practice course. The OIC of the range presents a tactical situation, and unfuzed practice hand grenades are issued to the platoon for the practice portion of the course. The OIC inspects all personnel before they negotiate the course to make certain that all grenades are properly secured. The OIC determines whether to issue grenades to the soldiers in the holding area or at the throwing bunker, depending upon their experience and proficiency.

(c) The first squad moves in line formation, ALPHA team on the right, from a tree line that represents the final coordination line of the practice course.

(d) Upon arrival at a mound representing the initial holding area, the squad is taken under fire by a machine gun simulator. The squad leader sends two men from the right side of the line to bunker number one near the objective. One man lays down a base-of-fire at target area number three. The safety officer directs the number-one man on the right to move to bunker number two within hand grenade range of the objective. From bunker number two, the soldier continues to fire his weapon until all far targets are suppressed. He then observes target area number one and engages it with a practice hand grenade. When the grenade is thrown, the safety officer commands ALL DOWN. This command pertains to everyone in the training area. At this time, all personnel get behind protective cover. After the grenade functions, the safety officer counts to seven, which indicates the amount of time personnel must remain behind the protective cover. The soldier engages target area number two with a second practice hand grenade. When the grenade is thrown, the safety officer commands ALL DOWN.

(e) The soldier who threw the grenades moves by the most direct route back to the final holding area where the critique NCO critiques him. Covering fire is continued from bunker number one. The squad leader then sends a new man to bunker number one where he provides covering fire as the number-two man moves to bunker number two to throw his grenades. After the second grenade functions, the soldier being critiqued by the critique NCO moves directly to the initial holding area.

(f) The above sequence is repeated until all squad personnel have thrown grenades and provided covering fire. The first soldier to throw grenades provides covering fire for the last man to throw.

(g) After the first group has finished the practice course and critique, the group returns to the assembly area and then moves to the live course area for the final run with fragmentation grenades. After the first group has completed the practice course, the practice and live courses are run concurrently on separate training areas.

NOTE: On the practice course, blank rifle ammunition and practice grenades are used. Live ammunition and two live grenades are used in the conduct of the live course. The safety officer must make sure the soldiers remove the blank adapters before issuing ammunition.

(h) The safety officer on the practice course carefully observes the actions of the soldiers throwing practice grenades. If the safety officer detects any unsafe acts or extreme nervousness on a thrower's part, the thrower is identified to the critique NCO. The critique NCO points out the thrower's mistakes and sends him back through the practice course. In some instances, it may be necessary to place an individual who has extreme difficulty in properly handling grenades under the control of an assistant instructor for detailed instruction. Under no circumstances can a man be allowed to throw live fragmentation grenades until he has clearly demonstrated his ability to throw practice grenades during the practice portion of the course.

(2) *Safety personnel.* The following safety personnel are required for the hand grenade confidence course:

(a) Officer in charge. The OIC or NCOIC (E7 or above) is responsible for the overall conduct of the training, the bleacher orientation, and the tactical briefing. After the OIC or NCOIC issues the operation order in the assembly area, the safety officer is positioned in the safety bunker where he has the immediate responsibility of supervising hand grenade throwing.

(b) Squad leaders. The squad leaders alternate moving squads to and from the initial holding areas. They are responsible for ensuring that all personnel are behind protective cover in the initial holding area when grenades are being thrown. Squad leaders must check each soldier's grenades before he moves from the initial holding area to bunker number one.

(c) Safety officer. The safety officer is the senior assistant instructor. He must be an E6 or above. Positioned in bunker number one, he controls the movement of all personnel both before and after each grenade is thrown. He also controls the soldier furnishing covering fire.

(d) Critique NCO. The critique NCO is positioned in the final holding area. He critiques each thrower immediately after the soldier arrives from bunker number two. To ensure continuity, the critique NCO observes the same squad during both the practice and live courses. He then returns to the practice course to observe another squad.

(3) *Training facility.* The training facility for the hand grenade confidence course consists of a practice grenade course for throwing the M69 practice grenades and a live grenade course for throwing fragmentation grenades. These two courses are constructed alike and close together to allow easy movement from one to the other. The hand grenade confidence course should be conducted concurrently with another 2-hour period of instruction in order to reduce terrain and personnel requirements. The breakdown for the conduct of training is as follows:

(a) Initial orientation (20 minutes).

(b) Tactical situation briefing, ammunition issue, and inspection before crossing the final coordination line (10 minutes).

(c) Practice run (35 minutes). Practice and live runs are done concurrently after the first squad completes the practice run.

(4) *Ammunition.* Each soldier needs 40 rounds of blank 5.56-mm ammunition, 40 rounds of live 5.56-mm ammunition, two M69 fuzed practice grenades, and two M67 fragmentation grenades. For each demonstration, 40 rounds of blank 5.56-mm ammunition and 2 fuzed practice hand grenades are required.

(5) *Ranges*. The range used for the confidence course consists of two separate areas, each consisting of an assembly area, a final coordination line, an initial holding area, a covering position, a throwing position, a safety officer's observation point, a final holding area, and two target areas.

(a) Assembly area. This area is used as a briefing point and an ammunition issue point. It should be a cleared area large enough to accommodate a 48- to 60-man platoon.

(b) Final coordination line. This line should be a prominent terrain feature, such as a wood line or streambed, located between the assembly area and the objective. Ideally, the area between the final coordination line and the objective should slope uphill. This is the last location outside the surface danger zone where personnel may maneuver freely without the need for cover to protect soldiers from fragmentation danger.

(c) Initial holding area. This area should be located 30 to 50 meters forward of the final coordination line. The area should be a mound or a roadside ditch that is long enough to accommodate nine men and high enough to afford protection for a kneeling man.

(d) Covering position. This position should be a mound or parapet 2 meters high and 8 meters wide across its front side. The position should be 5 meters forward of the right flank of the initial holding area.

(e) Throwing position. This position should be a mound or a parapet 1.5 meters high and 2 meters wide. The position should be located about 15 meters to the left front of the covering position.

(f) Observation point. This is the safety officer's observation point. It should be a pit affording the minimum frontal protection. The position is located 10 meters to the rear of the throwing position.

(g) Final holding area. This area should have characteristics similar to the initial holding area. The position must accommodate at least two kneeling men. It is located 5 meters to the left of the safety officer's observation point.

(h) Targets. There are three separate target areas in each course, practice and live. The target areas on the practice confidence course should be clearly marked practice targets.

- Target area 1 is the impact area for the first hand grenade. The target should be a cluster of half-inch steel E-type silhouette targets located at ranges varying from 25 to 40 meters.
- Target area 2 is the impact area for the second grenade. The target consists of a cluster of ten half-inch steel E-type silhouettes. This target should be unmarked and located at ranges varying from 25 to 40 meters and 50 meters to the left of target area one.
- Target area 3 is the target area for M16 fire. The target consists of a cluster of 15 to 20 pop-up E-type silhouettes located 50 to 100 meters from bunkers one and two.

(6) *Training area (general)*. The training area should be located on slightly sloping terrain. As much natural vegetation as possible should be left on the site.

4-3. COLLECTIVE TRAINING

Two aspects of preparing for combat are training and rehearsal. When training collective tasks or rehearsing a certain combat mission, noncommissioned officers analyze the collective tasks that are to be trained and select the individual tasks that support the collective tasks. They must then integrate the individual tasks into training and rehearsals. Applicable guidelines for planning collective tasks are as follows:

a. Training managers decide which collective tasks they must practice by analyzing the operation outlines contained in the appropriate mission training plan. The operation outlines detail the collective tasks required to execute a critical wartime mission. Noncommissioned officers find the individual tasks that support the collective tasks by referring to the mission task matrix in the appropriate platoon mission training plan. They find the correct training standards in the appropriate soldier's manual task. They use the squad and platoon MTP (ARTEP 7-8-MTP) and FM 7-8 to see how to use the individual tasks to do their collective tasks.

b. As an example, the team leader learns that his platoon is going to practice for an attack training mission. He analyzes the mission outline for attack and determines which collective tasks his squad may have to do as part of this mission. Several of these tasks require soldiers to engage in close combat.

c. Soldiers can use hand grenades anytime they engage the enemy in close combat. Collective tasks that require close combat are Conduct Fire and Movement, Disengage, Knock Out Bunker, Clear a Trench, Conduct a Near Ambush, Defend, and Clear a Building. Drills that require close combat are React to Contact, Break Contact, and React to Ambush. When units train or rehearse these tasks, they should also train and evaluate the use of hand grenades. Once soldiers can safely arm and throw live fragmentation hand grenades, units should integrate the use of grenades into collective tasks rather than training it as a separate event. Use simulation or live hand grenades, as appropriate, against realistic targets while practicing the collective tasks. Noncommissioned officers tell soldiers when and how to use the grenades, evaluate their use, correct mistakes, and retrain soldiers as necessary.

4-4. SAMPLE SQUAD SITUATIONAL TRAINING EXERCISE

Present soldiers with tactical situations in an STX requiring hand grenade use in conjunction with other fire team or squad weapons that force soldiers to make sound tactical decisions on hand grenade employment.

a. The STX should be a realistic training event that improves the soldier's hand grenade throwing skills, the use of his individual weapon, and the collective skills of his fire team and squad.

b. There are no firm guidelines for an STX (Figure 4-9). Consider hand grenade tasks in the tactical scenario that are best suited to the unit's METL. The close combat tasks listed in paragraph 4-3c should also be offered in a unit's STX training program. Soldiers should carry practice hand grenades whenever they carry their individual weapons. They should be required to use both to increase their individual abilities. The use of opposing forces enhances training realism. Opposing force objectives for specific actions can be found in ARTEP 7-8-MTP.

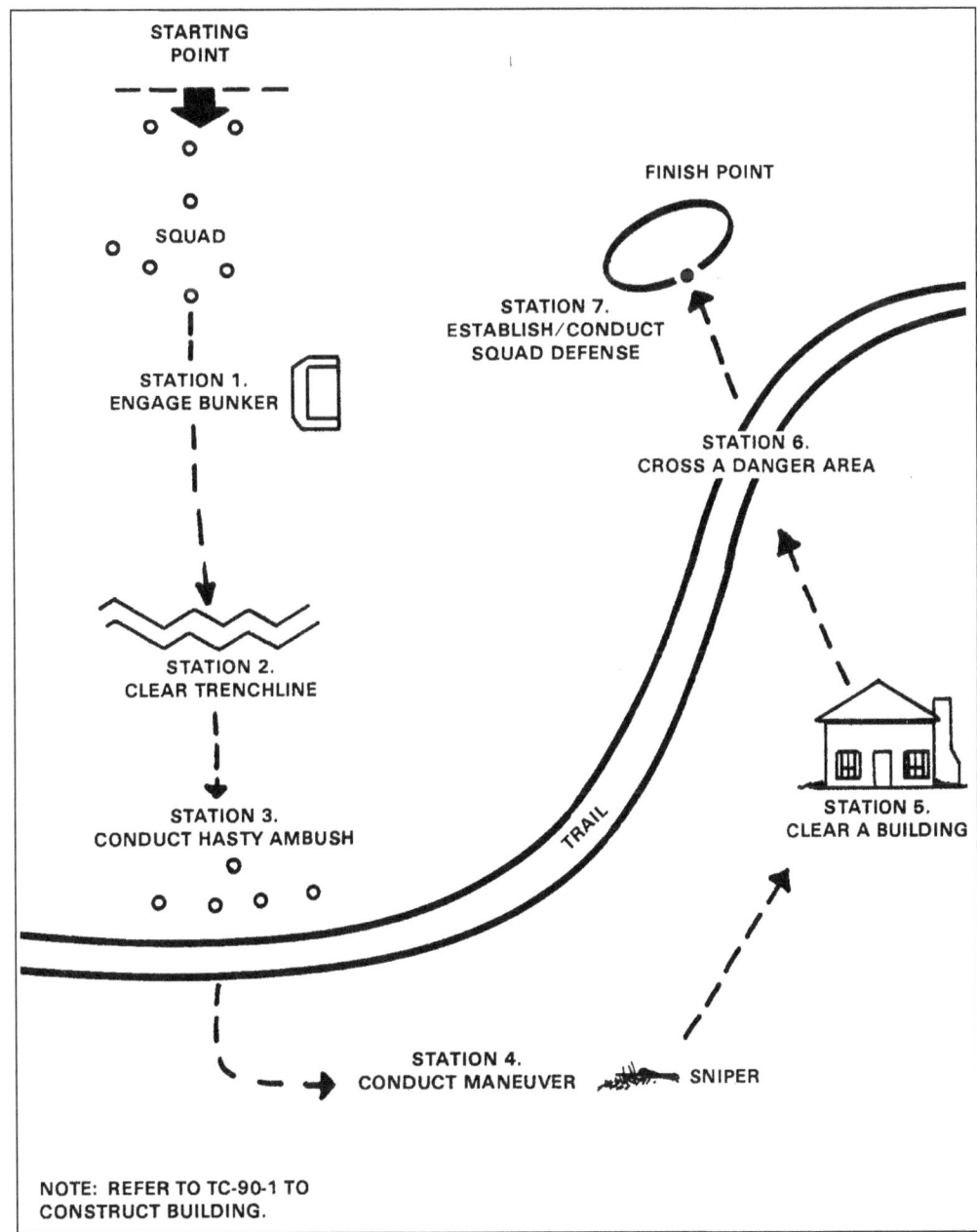

Figure 4-9. Example squad STX with hand grenades.

CHAPTER 5
GROUND PYROTECHNIC SIGNALS

Ground pyrotechnic signals are classified as either handheld or ground smoke signals. They are used for signaling and illuminating missions.

5-1. DESCRIPTION
Ground pyrotechnic signals rise to a height of 180 to 250 meters before functioning, unlike the old smoke grenades that functioned either on impact or shortly after firing. There are two types of pyrotechnic signals:

a. **Handheld Signals**. These signals are issued in their own launching mechanism and are designed to reach a minimum height of 200 meters. This group of signals includes five-star clusters, single-star parachutes, and smoke parachutes. Handheld signals have replaced all rifle-projected pyrotechnic signals and chemical grenades.

b. **Ground Smoke Signals**. These signals are self-contained units used by ground soldiers to signal aircraft or to convey information through a prearranged signal. The signal consists of a cylindrical smoke pellet, a fuze (thermalite-type ignitacord), an igniter cap, an internal retaining ring, and a striker ring assembled in an aluminum photocan container. These signals produce a smoke cloud that lasts 13 to 30 seconds. They replace rifle-projected smoke signals.

5-2. CAPABILITIES AND USES
Ground pyrotechnic signals are capable of signaling for communication or illuminating a small area.

a. **Communication**. Effective control of units on the battlefield depends largely on communication. Radio, telephone, voice, messenger, and arm-and-hand signals are communication means that may be ineffective in certain tactical situations. Pyrotechnic signals are used in such situations to supplement or to take the place of normal communication means. Pyrotechnic signals are prescribed at command level and are prearranged in accordance with SOPs.

b. **Illumination**. The illumination capabilities of pyrotechnic signals are somewhat limited because of their size. They can be used, however, to light a small area for short periods when two or more illuminating signals are used at the same time.

5-3. HANDHELD SIGNALS
Star clusters, star parachutes, and smoke parachutes are three handheld signals used by the Army.

a. **Star Clusters**. Star clusters are used for signaling and illuminating. They are issued in an expendable launcher, which consists of a launching tube and firing cap (1, 2, 3, and 4, Figure 5-1). These signals produce a cluster of five free-falling pyrotechnic stars, clusters, and smoke parachutes.

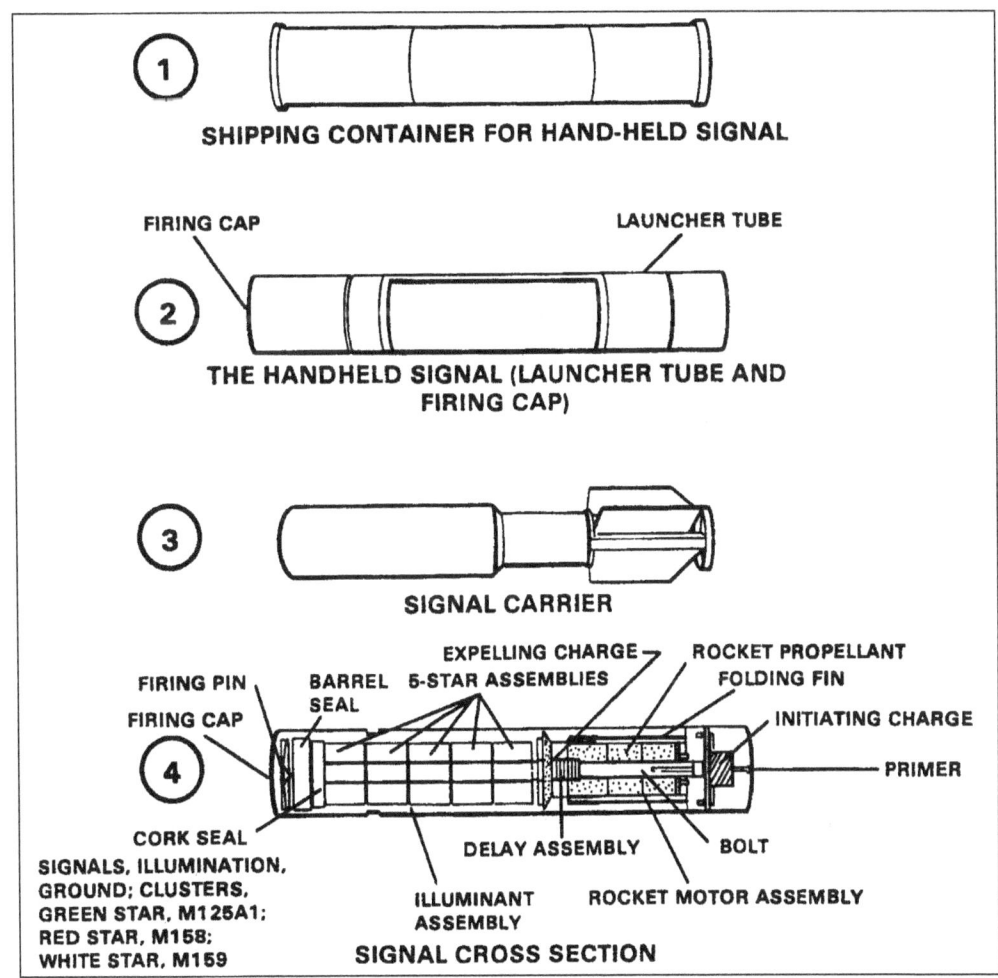

Figure 5-1. Ground pyrotechnic signals.

(1) *Types.* The current types of star clusters include the M125 and M125A1 (green star), the M158 (red star), and the M159 (white star).

(2) *Operation.* Operation of handheld signals should be as follows: (This will not always agree with the instructions found on the launcher tube. For more detailed information on safety and precautions, refer to TM 9-1370-206-10.)

(a) Hold the signal in your left hand, red-knurled band down, with your little finger in alignment with the red band (Figure 5-2).

(b) Withdraw the firing cap from the upper end of the signal.

(c) Point the ejection end of the signal away from your body and slowly push the firing cap onto the signal until the open end of the cap is aligned with the red band.

(d) Grasp the center of the signal firmly with your left hand, holding your elbow tight against your body with the signal at the desired trajectory angle and the firing cap at the bottom. Turn your head down and away from the signal to avoid injury to your face and eyes from particles ejected by the small rockets (Figure 5-2).

(e) Strike the bottom of the cap a sharp blow with the palm of your right hand or strike it on a hard surface, keeping your left arm rigid.

NOTE: Before firing the signal, the firer must make sure there is enough overhead clearance.

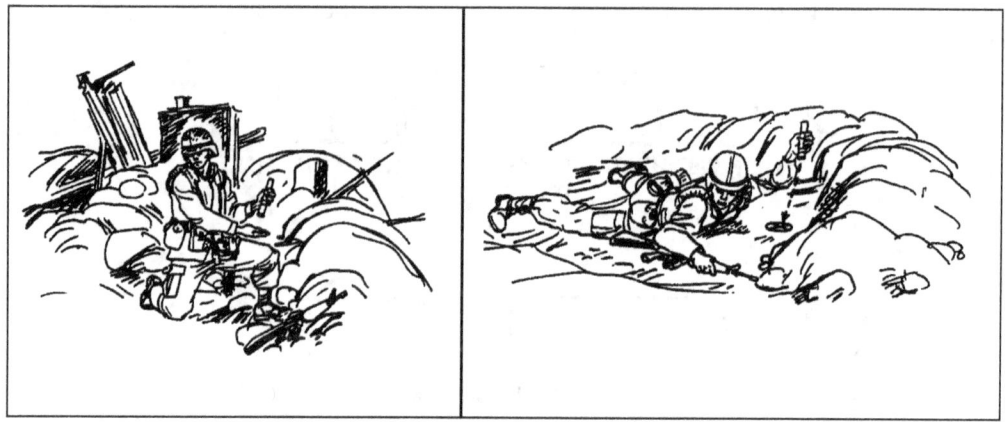

Figure 5-2. Firing the handheld signal.

(3) *Function.* When the firing cap is struck, the firing pin is forced into the base of the launcher tube at the primer. When the primer is struck, the flash from the primer ignites an initiating charge of black powder at the base of the signal. Gases from the burning initiating charge expel the signal from the launcher (rocket barrel) with a slight recoil. As the signal is expelled, four flexible steel fins unfold to stabilize the signal during flight. After the signal rises about 6 meters, the rocket motor, which was ignited by the propelling gases, begins to burn fully, forcing the signal to a height of 200 to 215 meters. At that point, a delay element ignites an ejection charge, which in turn forces the five-star illumination cluster out of the nose of the signal body.

(4) *Firing data.* Star clusters burn 6 to 10 seconds. Their rate of descent is 14 meters each second.

b.   **Star Parachutes**. Star parachutes are also used for signaling and illuminating. They are issued in an expendable launcher that consists of a launching tube and a firing cap. These signals produce a single parachute-suspended illuminant star.

(1) *Types.* The current types of star parachutes include the M126A1 (red star), the M127A1 (white star), and the M195 (green star).

(2) *Operation.* These signals are fired in the same manner as the star clusters.

(3) *Function.* These signals function in the same manner as the star clusters.

(4) *Firing data.* The M126- and M127-series star parachutes rise to a height of 200 to 215 meters. The M126 burns for 50 seconds, and the M127 burns for 25 seconds. The average rate of descent for either is 2.1 meters each second. The signals can be seen for 50 to 58 kilometers at night.

c.   **Smoke Parachutes**. Smoke parachutes are for signaling only. They are issued in an expendable launcher that consists of a launching tube and a firing cap. These signals produce a single perforated colored smoke canister that is parachute-suspended.

(1) *Types*. The current types of smoke parachutes include the M128A1 (green smoke), the M129A1 (red smoke), and the M194 (yellow smoke).

(2) *Operation*. These signals are fired in the same manner as the star clusters.

(3) *Function*. These signals function in the same manner as the star clusters.

(4) *Firing data*. Smoke parachutes rise to a height of 200 to 215 meters. The signals emit smoke for 6 to 18 seconds, forming a smoke cloud that persists for 60 seconds. Their rate of descent is 4 meters each second.

5-4. SURFACE TRIP FLARES

Surface trip flares outwardly resemble antipersonnel mines or hand grenades (Figure 5-3). Their primary use is to warn of infiltrating troops by illuminating the field. They are also used as signals or booby traps. The flares produce 50,000 candlepower of illumination.

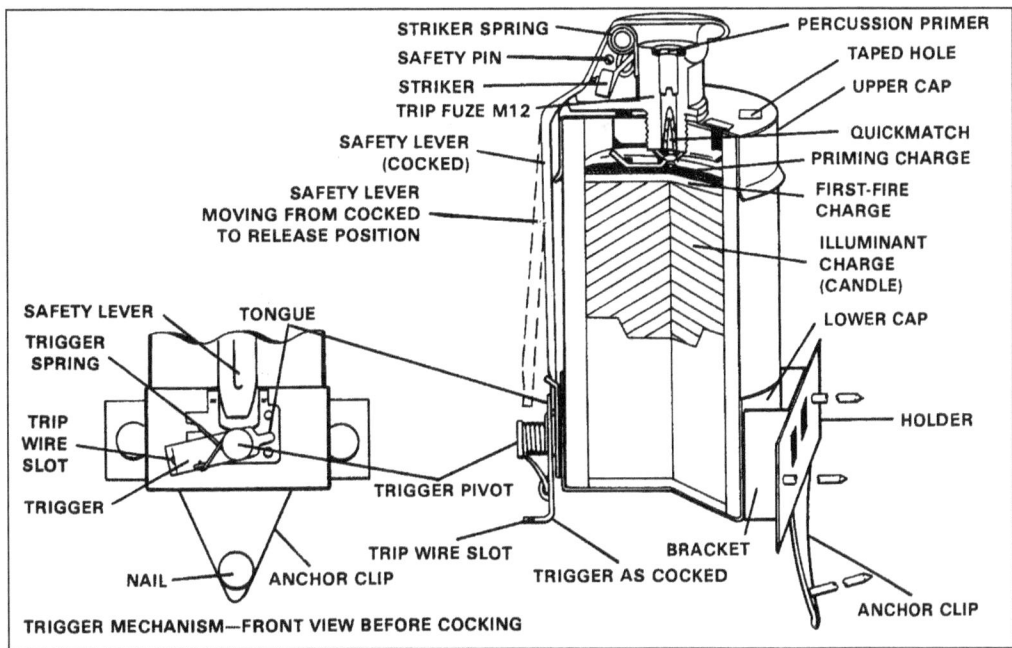

Figure 5-3. Surface trip flares.

5-5. SIMULATORS

Simulators are used in training to imitate the sounds and effects of combat detonations.

a. The booby trap simulator, M117, (Figure 5-4) is used during training and military exercises. This device allows training in the installation and use of booby traps. When tripped or activated, the simulator functions with a flash and loud report.

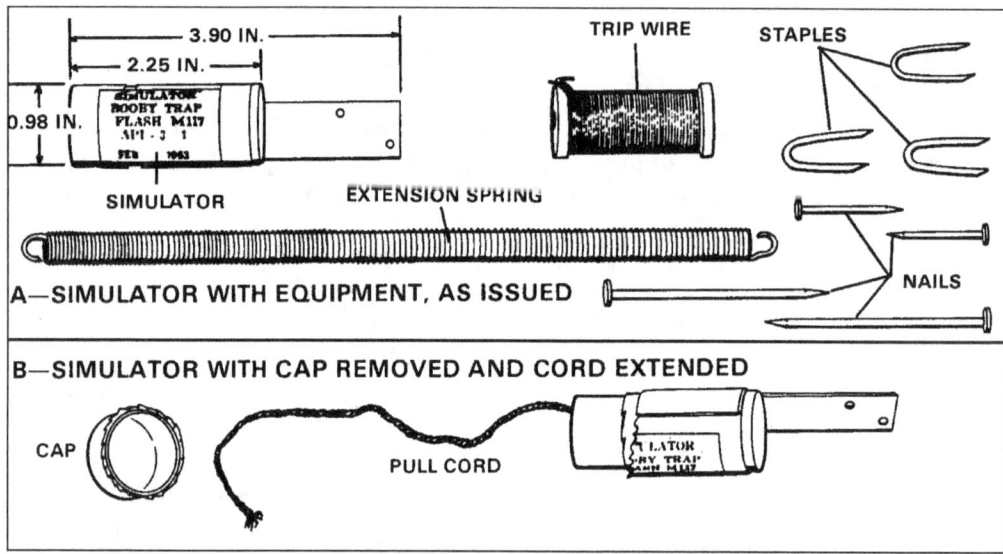

Figure 5-4. M117 simulator.

b. The ground burst simulator, M115A2, (Figure 5-5) is used to create battle noises and flash effects during training. It produces a high-pitched whistle that lasts 2 to 4 seconds. The detonation produces a flash and loud report.

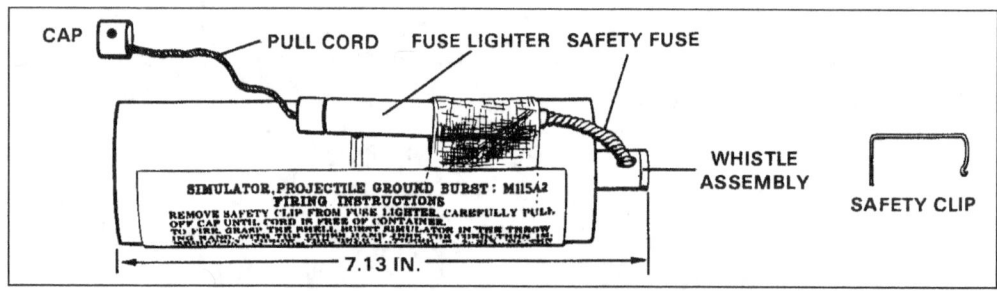

Figure 5-5. M115A2 simulator.

c. The hand grenade simulator, M116A1, (Figure 5-6) is used to create battle noises and flashes during training. It differs from the ground burst simulator in that it is shorter and does not emit a high-pitched whistle before detonation. The hand grenade simulator is thrown in the same manner as a live grenade. It creates a flash and loud report 5 to 10 seconds after ignition.

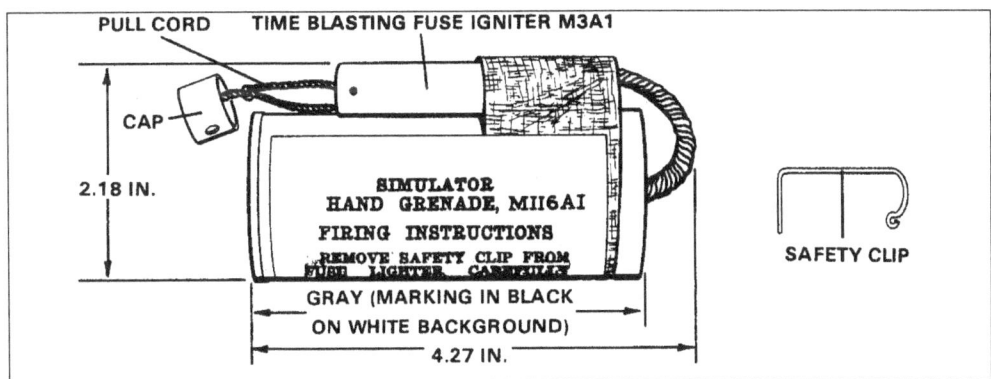

Figure 5-6. M116A1 simulator.

d. The explosive simulator, M80, (Figure 5-7) is used during training and in deactivation training programs. It simulates hand grenades, booby traps, land mines, and rifle or artillery fire.

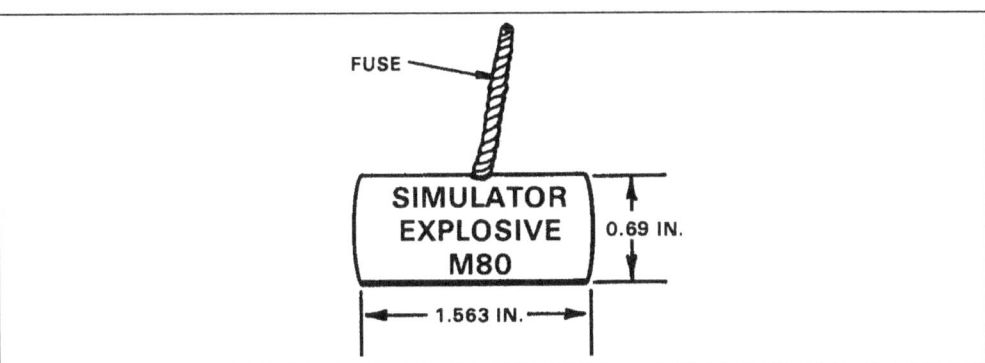

Figure 5-7. M80 simulator.

5-6. ILLUMINATION GROUND SIGNAL KITS

The pen gun flare supports the small unit leader in fire control, maneuver, and initiating operations such as ambushes.

a. **Kit 1**. This pen gun flare has a threaded projector with the projectiles contained in a cloth bandoleer. Each of the signals listed below may be fired from a handheld projector while in a bandoleer.

- Red illumination ground signal, M187.
- White illumination ground signal, M188.
- Green illumination ground signal, M189.
- Amber illumination ground signal, M190.

(1) *Contents*. The projector and the bandoleer plus seven projectiles or signals make up the signal kit (Figure 5-8). All signals may be obtained and fired separately. The M185 red signal kit contains only red signals. The M186 signal kit contains three red, two white, and two green signals.

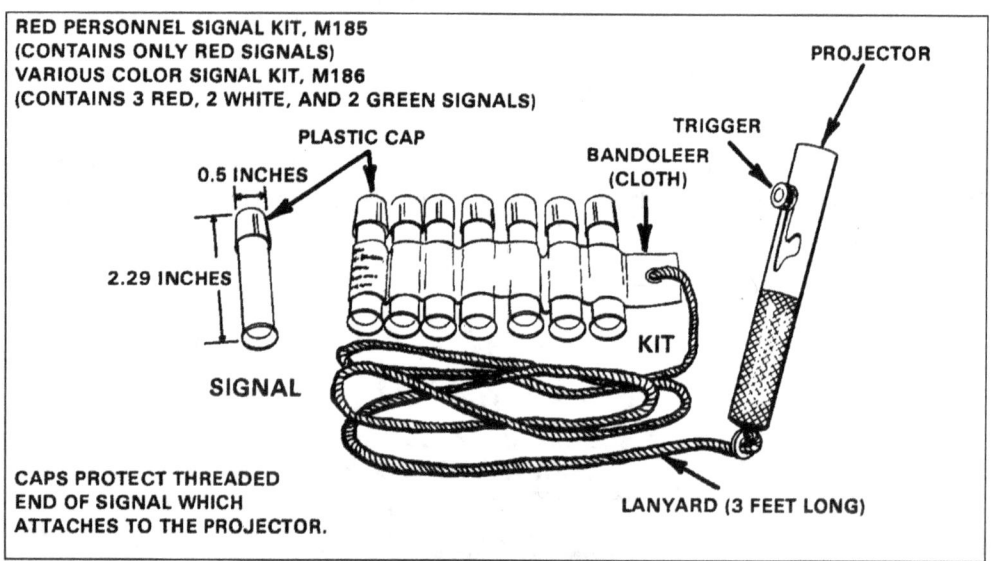

Figure 5-8. Signal kit 1.

(2) *Operation*. Select the signal to be fired by color. If the bandoleer contains more than one signal of the chosen color, use the one farthest from the lanyard. Remove and discard the plastic cap. Cock the projector by moving the trigger to the safety slot. Carefully thread the projector onto the signal, taking care not to dislodge the trigger from the safety slot. Aim in the chosen direction. Fire by moving the trigger to the bottom of the slot and releasing it with a snap. If the expended signal is on the end of the bandoleer or if the signals between the expended signal and the end have been used, cut the bandoleer and discard the waste. Return the partly used kit to the barrier bag and seal with tape.

b. **Kit 2**. This pen gun flare has a force-fitted projector and a plastic bandoleer before being fired.

(1) *Contents*. This kit contains only red illumination ground signals. The projector and the bandoleer plus seven signals make up this kit (Figure 5-9). The burning time for these signals is 10 seconds at 100,000 candlepower.

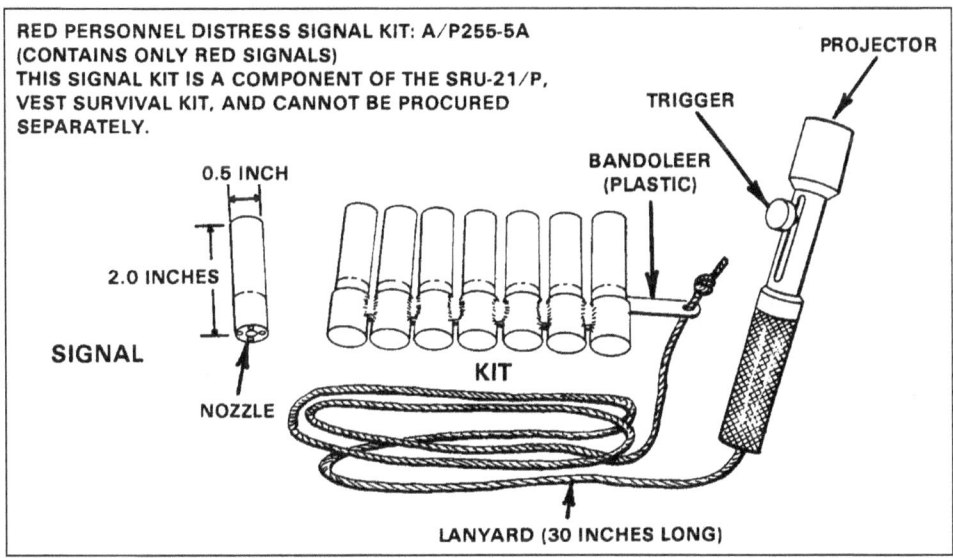

RED PERSONNEL DISTRESS SIGNAL KIT: A/P255-5A
(CONTAINS ONLY RED SIGNALS)
THIS SIGNAL KIT IS A COMPONENT OF THE SRU-21/P,
VEST SURVIVAL KIT, AND CANNOT BE PROCURED
SEPARATELY.

PROJECTOR
TRIGGER
BANDOLEER
(PLASTIC)
0.5 INCH
2.0 INCHES
SIGNAL
KIT
NOZZLE
LANYARD (30 INCHES LONG)

Figure 5-9. Signal kit 2.

(2) *Operation*. To operate this signal, select and remove the signal to be fired from the bandoleer using the one farthest from the lanyard. Carefully insert the nozzle end of the signal into the projector as far as it will go. Fire by pulling the trigger knob to the rear of the slot and releasing it with a snap. Retain the bandoleer for future use. Return the partly used kit to the plastic bag and seal with tape.

LIVE HAND GRENADE RANGE OPERATIONS CHECKLIST

This appendix is designed to assist leaders in the safe operation of a basic live hand grenade range. As a checklist, it does not provide the answers but asks the questions for leaders to answer. Modification of the checklist for other types of live hand grenade training (collective training, STX, and so forth) is expected. The following is a suggested checklist:

A-1. BECOME AN EXPERT
- Review written material.
- Review AR 385-63.
- Review FM 23-30 and TM 9-1330-200-12.
- Check out the range.
- Visit range control and read installation range instructions.

A-2. DETERMINE REQUIREMENTS
- Personnel.
- OIC.
- Safety officer.
- Assistant safety officer.
- NCOIC.
- Ammunition personnel.
- Target detail.
- Tower operator.
- Assistant instructors.
- RATELOs.
- Guards, as required.
- Aidmen, with required medical supplies.
- Truck driver.

A-3. EQUIPMENT
- Kevlar, body armor, LCE, and earplugs issued to all personnel, instructors, and students.
- Range packet and clearance form.
- Safety fan and diagram.
- Appropriate publications pertaining to training (FMs, TMs, ARs).
- Lesson plans, status reports, and reporting folders.
- Range flag.
- Communications equipment to include a phone, FM radios, and field radios; two means of communication are required.
- PA system with bullhorns for backup.

- Kevlars marked for control personnel.
- Ambulance or required dedicated evacuation vehicle; the driver must have knowledge of the route to the hospital.
- Earplugs for all personnel; have extras on hand for visitors.
- Water for drinking and cleaning.
- Qualification scorecards.
- Tables and chairs, if needed.
- Training aids.
- Targets required for the operation of the range (bunkers or personnel targets 1/4-inch steel E-type silhouette).

A-4. OCCUPY, INSPECT, AND SET UP RANGE
- Establish good communication by at least two means.
- Have designated parking areas for cadre and training unit personnel.
- Have secured ammunition points.
- Establish locations for medical station.
- Establish water points.
- Have a designated mess area.
- Have a designated helipad.
- Inspect range for operational conditions.
- Make sure the impact area is raked and clear of debris.
- Check all throwing pits for sharp edges or unleveled throwing surfaces.
- Check to ensure knee walls meet standards.
- Check tower and tower PA system.
- Raise the red flag when occupying or firing, according to local SOP.
- Request an opening code from range control.

A-5. PREPARATION FOR TRAINING
- Get a good head count of all soldiers going to train.
- Identify soldiers who will not be training.
- Issue equipment and ammunition necessary to conduct training.
- Conduct safety briefing to include administrative personnel.
- Organize personnel into throwing orders.

A-6. CONDUCT INITIAL HAND GRENADE TRAINING
- Move soldiers to training location.
- Issue practice grenades to soldiers.
- Show soldiers inspection procedures when unpacking hand grenades.
- Show soldiers composure of grenade, for example, body, fuze, and three safeties.
- Teach soldiers proper left and right handgrips.
- Teach soldiers proper throwing positions and techniques.
- Let soldiers practice throwing grenades, 10 or more as required for efficiency.

A-7. INSPECTION OF LIVE HAND GRENADES
- Open the canister and visually inspect the grenade.
- If grenade is packed upside down, turn in grenade. (See TM 9-1330-200-12.)
- If safety pin or safety clip is missing, turn in grenade.
- If all the above is in order, remove grenade from canister.
- If grenade body is cracked, turn in grenade.
- If fuze lugs are broken, turn in grenade.
- If safety lever is bent or broken, turn in grenade.
- The safety pin must have either a diamond crimp or a 45-degree spread; if not, turn in grenade (TM 9-1330-200-12).
- If pull ring is cracked, turn in grenade.
- If fuze is loose, turn in grenade.

A-8. MOVEMENT TO LIVE-BAY TRAINING AREA
Soldiers are briefed to prepare to move down to the live-bay throwing site. Individual weapons and protective masks are grounded in the designated training unit area of operation. Range cadre ensure soldiers have earplugs, flak vest, LCE, and Kevlar. Soldiers also ensure that all equipment is properly worn and fastened. Before marching the soldiers to the live-bay site, a last minute check is made to make sure any high-risk soldier is identified in the initial training period and is pulled out of the formation.

a. **Safety Precautions**.

(1) After soldiers go past the prescribed roadblocks and or barriers, make sure a guard is posted and briefed on procedures for individuals wanting to cross roadblocks during live throwing of grenades.

(2) Communication between roadblock and tower must be confirmed before live throwing.

(3) Soldiers are shown the live-bay training area and a safety briefing is given on the operating procedures of live bay. Cadre reinforce the fact that cooking-off and milking of hand grenades are not allowed in live bay. Soldiers are also briefed on the procedures for dropping grenades.

(4) After the live-bay safety briefing, march the soldiers to the overhead cover area.

(5) Soldiers are checked once more to ensure all have earplugs and equipment is properly secured.

b. **Issue of Live Hand Grenades**.

(1) Issue grenades to the soldiers making sure they are holding the grenades using a proper left or right handgrip. Grenades are issued only to those soldiers who are next in line to go to the throwing pit. The safety NCO makes sure the soldiers are holding the grenades properly and at the chin-chest level.

(2) When departing to the live-bay pit, the safety officer directs soldiers to sound off, each indicating with which hand he will throw the grenade.

A-9. THROWING OF LIVE HAND GRENADES

Throwing of live hand grenades can be done in a safe manner if the range safety procedures are followed. These procedures include identification of high-risk soldiers as well as reinforcement of training to those soldiers who may have had problems during the initial training block of instruction. Live-bay cadre must be completely alert at all times and prepared to take appropriate actions for any given situation. The following is guidance for operation procedures of live-bay throwing.

- The range OIC must be positioned in the tower to observe the throw phase and count grenade explosions for purposes of grenade accountability and duds.
- A pit NCO is assigned to each throwing pit.
- The safety NCO issuing grenades directs soldiers to specific throwing pits.
- The pit safety NCO observes movement of soldiers to the pit.
- The soldier identifies the throwing arm to the pit safety NCO.
- The pit safety NCO directs the soldier to the appropriate position of the pit, based on left or right throwing arm.
- The pit NCO directs the soldier to hand over the grenade in his nonthrowing hand.
- The pit safety NCO directs the soldier to remove the safety clip and prepare to throw. From this point on, the pit safety NCO does not remove his eyes from the throwing hand until completion of the throw. The pit safety NCO signals the tower that the soldier is prepared to throw by holding up his left or right arm in a vertical position.

WARNING

If a grenade is dropped in the pit, the pit safety NCO forces the soldier out of the pit into the designated safe area and follows him.

A-10. ORDER TO THROW FROM TOWER

- When all throwing pits are ready, the tower NCO commands THROW, and the pit NCO repeats the THROW command to the soldier in the pit.
- All pits throw at the same time.
- The soldiers throw the grenades, then drop to cover. If the soldier does not take cover, the pit NCO forces the soldier to take cover if needed.
- The tower NCO commands CLEAR after observing each grenade detonate.
- The soldiers prepare to throw a second grenade, repeating the required steps.

> **WARNING**
> If a soldier releases the safety lever but fails to throw the grenade, the pit safety NCO forcefully repeats the command to throw; if necessary, the pit safety NCO grabs and throws the grenade himself.

A-11. COMPLETE THE TRAINING MISSION
- Clear the range.
- Close down the range in accordance with local SOP.
- Remove all equipment and ammunition from the range.
- Police the range, fill in all holes with sand, rake the impact area, and perform other range maintenance as required by local SOP.
- Request a range inspection from range control when ready to clear.
- Turn in paperwork and equipment.
- Submit after action report to headquarters.
- Report any noted safety hazards to proper authorities.
- Turn in all unexpended grenades in original grenade containers to the ASP, along with all safety pins and packing residue from all detonated grenades.

APPENDIX B
HAND GRENADE SAFETY CONSIDERATIONS

As simple as the fragmentation hand grenade may seem, it is a very powerful and dangerous weapon. Soldiers must understand the fatal effects that might take place with a hand grenade training accident. Since 1990, a number of fatal accidents have happened throughout training areas within the US. These training accidents have been recorded with basic training soldiers as well as seasoned soldiers within our armed forces. This appendix lists precautions and other considerations to be followed by hand grenade users. It should be used with Appendix A, Live Hand Grenade Range Operations Checklist, to educate leaders to safely conduct hand grenade training.

B-1. GENERAL PRECAUTIONS

Observe general precautions applicable to the use of any ammunition. More specific instructions to grenade users include the following:

a. Do not open the grenade containers or remove the protective devices until just before use.

b. Never make unauthorized modifications to hand grenades.

c. Do not remove the safety clip or the safety pin until the grenade is about to be thrown.

(1) A safety clip can be removed and reattached to a hand grenade if the safety pin is still in place.

(2) Never attempt to reinsert a safety pin into a bursting hand grenade during training. In combat, however, it may be necessary to reinsert a safety pin into a bursting grenade. Take special care to replace the pin properly. If the tactical situation allows, it is safer to throw the grenade rather than to trust the reinserted pin. Safety pins may be replaced in smoke and burning riot-control grenades.

B-2. TRAINING PRECAUTIONS

Treat any thrown grenade that fails to detonate as a dud, regardless of safety pin, safety clip, or safety lever status.

a. Know the status of the grenade.

(1) SAFE—a grenade with all safety devices intact.

(2) LIVE—a thrown grenade from the instant it is released until the expected fuze time has elapsed.

(3) DUD—a thrown grenade that failed to detonate after the expected fuze time has elapsed.

b. During training, the pit NCO determines a dropped grenade's status (safe, live, or dud).

c. Throwers must consider the flight path of the grenade to make sure no obstacles alter the flight of the grenade or cause it to bounce back toward them.

d. Make sure that the impact area is level and free of debris before throwing the casualty-producing hand grenade in training.

e. Do not handle, approach, recover, or otherwise tamper with dud grenades. Explosive ordnance disposal (EOD) personnel handle dud grenades.

f. Observe caution when using hand grenades with igniting type fuzes (M14-TH3, AN-M18, M7A2/A3, and AN-M83). These grenades ignite with a flash and should be thrown at least 10 meters from all personnel to avoid hazardous conditions.

B-3. DUDS

Duds must be regarded as dangerous. The following procedures must be followed if a grenade does not detonate:

a. **M69 Practice Grenade**. Wait 5 minutes before defuzing the M69 practice grenade. Keep the bottom of the grenade oriented in a safe area. Place the dud fuze in a sand-filled container and return it to the issuing facility.

b. **Fragmentation Grenade**. The thrower and supervisor wait in the throwing pit for 5 minutes before returning to a covered area. Notify EOD immediately. Do not throw any hand grenades into the area of the dud until it has been neutralized. If range facilities provide, continue training on adjacent impact area separated by berms.

B-4. DROPPED LIVE HAND GRENADES

If a casualty-producing grenade is dropped accidentally after the safety pin has been removed, the throwing pit safety NCO is responsible for reacting accordingly. He is responsible for the safety of the thrower, and he decides what actions are the most appropriate. His actions are dependent upon many factors, such as the safety design of the throwing pit, the location of the dropped grenade, the location of the thrower, and possibly his ability to physically move the thrower. All of these factors need to be considered before the safety pin is pulled.

a. **Throwing Pit With Knee Wall**. It is recommended that all throwing pits for live grenade training have knee walls (Figure B-1). Knee walls provide the quickest and safest means of reacting to a dropped grenade. In most instances, the throwing pit safety NCO reacts to a dropped live grenade by yelling GRENADE to alert all other personnel in the area and by physically pushing the thrower over the knee wall, then falling on top of him. If a hand grenade is dropped over the knee wall, the throwing pit safety NCO yells GRENADE and forces the thrower to the ground inside the throwing pit.

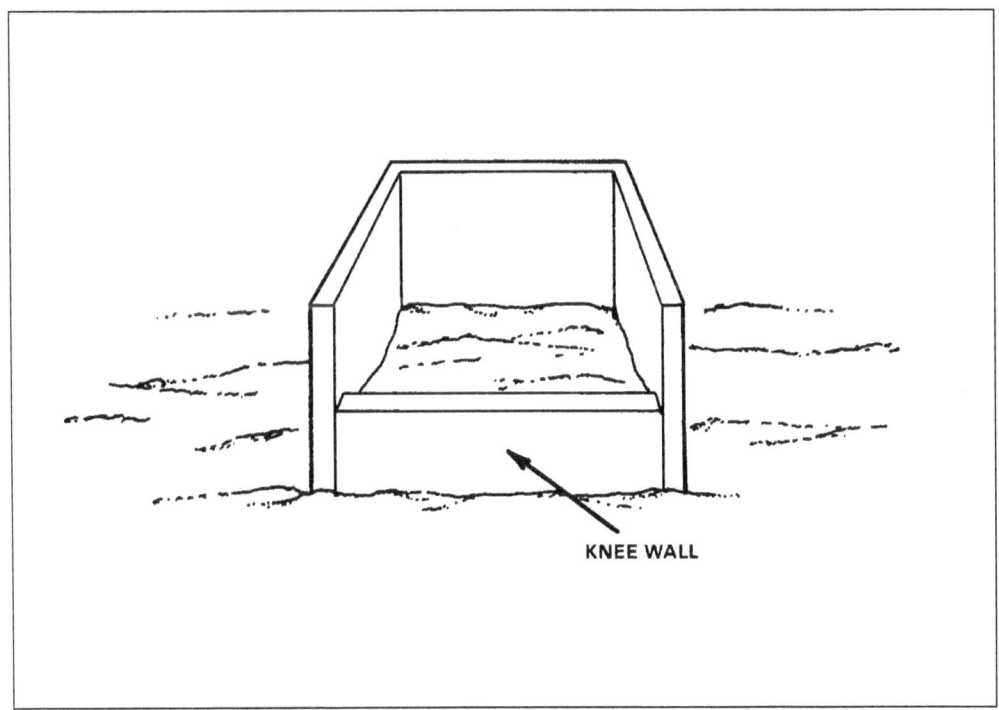

KNEE WALL

Figure B-1. Throwing pit with knee wall.

b. **Throwing Pit Without Knee Wall**. Throwing pits that do not have knee walls must have safety pits attached to both sides (Figure B-2). In most instances, the throwing pit safety NCO reacts to a dropped live grenade by yelling GRENADE to alert other personnel in the area and by physically moving the thrower out of the throwing pit and into a safety pit. If the hand grenade is dropped to the rear of the throwing pit, the throwing pit safety NCO yells GRENADE and forces the thrower over the front of the throwing pit. He follows the thrower over the wall. The safety NCO's first responsibility is the thrower's safety. His immediate action must be to remove the thrower from the danger area.

c. **Sumps**. Do not kick or throw grenades into sumps. In response to a dropped grenade, soldiers move from the danger area and drop to the prone position with Kevlars facing the direction of the grenade. This reduces the soldiers' exposure and increases the protection of the Kevlars.

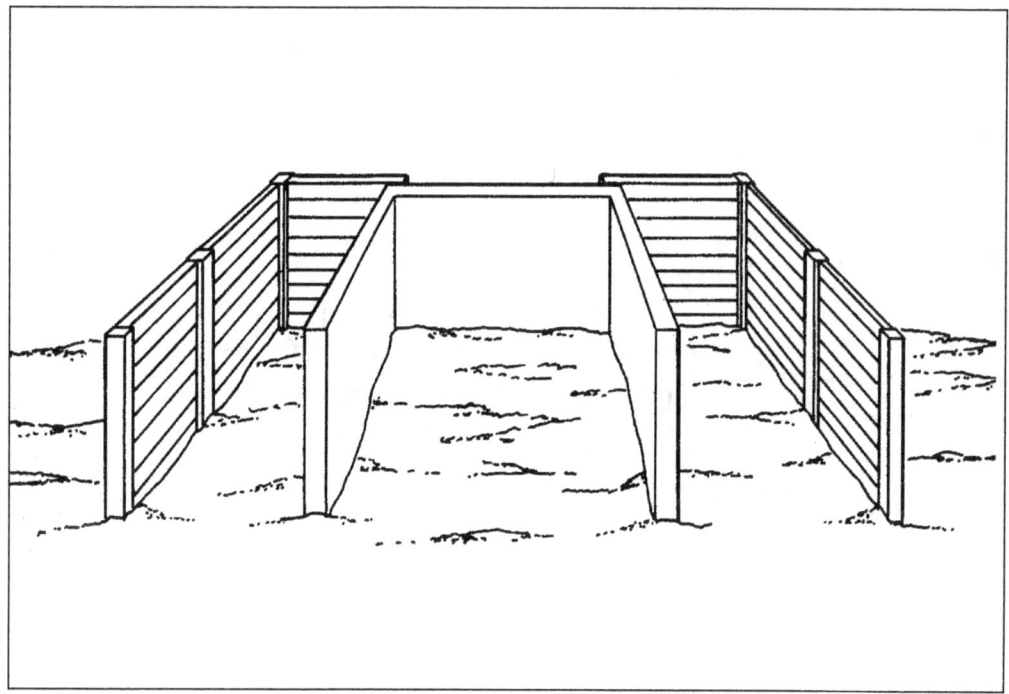

Figure B-2. Throwing pit with safety pits.

B-5. PROPER GRIP

Hold the safety lever firmly. An insufficient grip on the safety lever could result in the striker rotating and striking the primer that ignites the delay element. This can occur on most grenades without the safety lever being detached from the grenade.

B-6. HELICOPTERS

Do not throw fragmentation grenades from low flying or hovering helicopters. The fragments present a hazard to the aircraft and its passengers. Generally, throwing hand grenades from medium- or high-flying helicopters is limited to mission-critical situations.

B-7. AIRBORNE

During training missions, do not attach hand grenades on ammunition pouches during airborne operations. Carry the grenades in the main body of the rucksack instead. During wartime conditions, it is essential that soldiers are prepared to engage the enemy as soon as the chopper hits the ground; therefore, soldiers must carry their grenades in their ammunition pouches with the secondary safety removed. The following are suggested techniques to be used during training missions.

a. Before removing grenades from canisters, make sure inspection procedures are followed IAW TM 9-1330-200-12. Remove grenades from canisters and tape the safety pin and safety lever to the grenade. Fold back the tape for a quick release.

b. Return grenades to the canister for carrying. When taking out grenades, inspect them again to make sure tape and safeties are intact.

B-8. ENVIRONMENTAL PROTECTION

All leaders, trainers, and soldiers must comply with environmental laws and regulations. The leader must identify the environmental risks associated with training individual and collective tasks. Trainers must work to reduce and avoid damage to training areas and environment caused by realistic training. Environmental risk management parallels safety risk management and is based on the same philosophy. Environmental risk management consists of the following steps:

a. **Identify Hazards**. Identify the potential sources for environmental degradation during the analysis of METT-T factors. This requires identification of environmental hazards. An environmental hazard is a condition with the potential for polluting air, soil, or water or destroying cultural or historical artifacts.

b. **Assess Hazards**. Analyze the potential severity of environmental degradation by using the environmental risk assessment matrixes in FM 3-100.4 and the example risk management worksheet shown in Figure B-3. The severity of environmental degradation is considered when determining the potential effect an operation may have on the environment. The risk effect value is defined as an indicator of the severity of environmental degradation. Quantify the risk to the environment resulting from the operation as extremely high, medium, or low using the environmental assessment matrixes.

c. **Make Environmental Risk Decisions**. Make decisions and develop measures to reduce high environmental risks.

d. **Brief Chain of Command**. Brief the chain of command (to include installation environmental office, if applicable) on proposed plans and pertinent high-risk environmental matrixes. Risk decisions are made at a level of command that corresponds to the degree of risk.

e. **Implement Controls**. Implement environmental protection measures by integrating them into plans, orders, SOPs, training performance standards, and rehearsals.

f. **Supervise**. Supervise and enforce environmental protection standards.

RISK MANAGEMENT WORKSHEET

Operation/Training Event: MALONE 1 (HAND GRENADES)
Organization: A CO, 2/29th IN REGT

Date: RECURRING EVENT

Prepared by: SFC ROGERS

Page 1 of 9

HAZARD	INITIAL PROBABILITY	INITIAL EFFECT	INITIAL RISK LEVEL	CONTROLS IMPLEMENTED	RESIDUAL PROBABILITY	RESIDUAL EFFECT	RESIDUAL RISK LEVEL
1(A) RANGE/ GENERAL SITUATIONAL AWARENESS				**THE RANGE OFFICER IN CHARGE (OIC)/SAFETY OFFICER (RSO) WILL DO THE FOLLOWING:** 1. READ AND REVIEW THE RISK ASSESSMENT. 2. ENSURE CADRE COMBAT LIFESAVERS AND A DEDICATED EVACUATION VEHICLE ARE AVAILABLE. INVENTORY COMBAT LIFESAVER'S FIRST AID BAG OF THE TRAINING COMPANY. CONSULT WITH TRAINING COMPANY CADRE TO IDENTIFY PROBLEM SOLDIERS — SUICIDAL OR HOMICIDAL INTENT OR GESTURES, OR DEMONSTRATION OF SERIOUS EMOTIONAL ADJUSTMENTS. 3. IDENTIFY SOLDIERS WITH MEDICAL PROBLEMS HAVING THE POTENTIAL TO IMPACT TRAINING TO INCLUDE MINOR ILLNESSES, ALLERGIES, PREVIOUS HEAT AND/OR COLD WEATHER INJURIES, OR ENVIRONMENTAL SENSITIVITIES. 4. REVIEW EVACUATION PROCEDURES AND REPORTING PROCEDURES FOR SERIOUS INCIDENTS. PLAN TO EVACUATE SOLDIERS WITH ALLERGIC REACTIONS, ANYONE WITHIN 25 METERS OF A LIGHTNING STRIKE, COLD WEATHER/HEAT INJURIES, SNAKEBITE, OR ANYONE SHOWING SYMPTOMS BEYOND THE RANGE OIC'S EXPERIENCE AND THE COMBAT LIFESAVER'S ABILITY TO TREAT. THE OIC/RSO WILL DIRECT AN AIR MEDEVAC WHEN THE DANGER OF LOSS OF LIFE, LIMB, OR EYESIGHT EXISTS. 5. ASCERTAIN WHAT TYPE OF TRAINING THE UNIT HAS DONE FOR THE PREVIOUS 24 HOURS AND THE AVERAGE AMOUNT OF REST THE SOLDIERS HAVE BEEN ALLOWED. 6. CONDUCT DAILY RISK ASSESSMENT IN CONSULTATION WITH TRAINING COMPANY CADRE REPRESENTATIVES.			

INITIAL OVERALL RISK:

EXTREMELY HIGH	HIGH	MEDIUM	LOW

RESIDUAL OVERALL RISK:

EXTREMELY HIGH	**HIGH**	MEDIUM	LOW	**RISK ACCEPTANCE:** Type signature block, and sign.

ARDRELLE L. EVANS
CPT, IN
Commanding
FB Form 46-R, 20 Apr 95

GORDON B. DAVIS, JR.
LTC, IN
Commanding

RICHARD J. ROWE, JR.
COL, IN
Commanding

CARL F. ERNST
MAJOR GENERAL, USA
Commanding

Figure B-3. Example of risk management worksheet.

Figure B-3. Example of risk management worksheet (continued).

RISK MANAGEMENT WORKSHEET
CONTINUATION

Operation/Training Event: MALONE 1 (HAND GRENADES)
Organization: A CO, 2/29th IN REGT
Date: RECURRING EVENT

Prepared by: SFC ROGERS
Page 2 of 9

HAZARD	INITIAL PROBABILITY	INITIAL EFFECT	INITIAL RISK LEVEL	CONTROLS IMPLEMENTED	RESIDUAL PROBABILITY	RESIDUAL EFFECT	RESIDUAL RISK LEVEL
1(B). HEAT.	D REMOTE	I CATASTROPHIC	HIGH	(see below)	E UNLIKELY	I CATASTROPHIC	MEDIUM

CONTROLS IMPLEMENTED:

1. THE TRAINING UNIT WILL MONITOR WET BULB FOR HEAT CATEGORY. PREVIOUS HEAT INJURIES WILL BE MONITORED THROUGH THE BUDDY SYSTEM, TRAINING COMPANY CADRE, AND INSTRUCTORS

2. HEAT CATEGORIES WILL BE ENFORCED AS FOLLOWS:

HEAT CAT	WBGT INDEX F	EASY WORK	EASY WATER	MODERATE WORK	MODERATE WATER	HARD WORK	HARD WATER
1	78-81.9	NL	½	NL	¾	40/20	¾
2	82-84.9	NL	½	50/10	¾	30/30	1
3	85-87.9	NL	¾	40/20	¾	30/30	1
4	88-89.9	NL	¾	30/30	¾	20/40	1
5	>90	50/10	1	20/40	1	10/50	1

EASY WORK
• WEAPON MAINTENANCE
• WALKING HARD SURFACE AT 2.5 MPH, 30 LB LOAD
• MANUAL OF ARMS
• MARKSMANSHIP TRAINING
• DRILL AND CEREMONY

MODERATE WORK
• WALKING LOOSE SAND AT 2.5 MPH, NO LOAD
• WALKING HARD SURFACE AT 3.5 MPH, LESS THAN 40 LB LOAD
• CALISTHENICS
• PATROLLING
• INDIVIDUAL MOVEMENT TECHNIQUES, I.E., LOW CRAWL, HIGH CRAWL
• DEFENSIVE POSITION CONSTRUCTION
• FIELD ASSAULTS

HARD WORK
• WALKING HARD SURFACE AT 3.5 MPH, MORE THAN 40 LB LOAD
• WALKING LOOSE SAND AT 2.5 MPH WITH LOAD

3. DAILY WATER INTAKE SHOULD NOT EXCEED 12 QTS.

4. EVACUATE HEAT CASUALTIES IN ACCORDANCE WITH SERIOUS INCIDENT GUIDELINES/POST REQUIREMENTS.

FB Form 46-R, 20 Apr 95

Figure B-3. Example of risk management worksheet (continued).

RISK MANAGEMENT WORKSHEET
CONTINUATION

Operation/Training Event: MALONE 1 (HAND GRENADES)
Organization: A CO, 2/29th IN REGT

Date: RECURRING EVENT

Page 3 of 9
Prepared by: SFC ROGERS

HAZARD	INITIAL PROBABILITY	INITIAL EFFECT	INITIAL RISK LEVEL	CONTROLS IMPLEMENTED	RESIDUAL PROBABILITY	RESIDUAL EFFECT	RESIDUAL RISK LEVEL
1(C). COLD	E UNLIKELY	I CATASTROPHIC	MEDIUM	1. ALL SOLDIERS WITH PREVIOUS COLD INJURIES WILL BE IDENTIFIED AND CLOSELY MONITORED THROUGH THE BUDDY SYSTEM, TRAINING COMPANY CADRE, AND INSTRUCTORS. 2. **IMMERSION FOOT:** CAUSE: PROLONGED IMMERSION IN COLD WATER, USUALLY IN EXCESS OF 12 HOURS AT TEMPERATURES BELOW 50 DEGREES F. 3. **TRENCH FOOT:** CAUSE: EXPOSURE TO WETNESS AND COLD BETWEEN FREEZING AND 50 DEGREES FAHRENHEIT, LASTING HOURS TO SEVERAL DAYS. 4. **FROST BITE:** CAUSE: EXPOSURE TO COLD AT TEMPERATURES OF FREEZING OR BELOW, FOR MINUTES TO SEVERAL HOURS. 5. **HYPOTHERMIA:** CAUSE: HEAT LOSS EXCEEDING BODY'S HEAT PRODUCTION RESULTING IN BODY TEMPERATURE OF 95 DEGREES FAHRENHEIT OR LOWER. 6. **FIRST AID MEASURES:** REMOVE WET CLOTHING, REST AFFECTED PART AND REWARM IT PROMPTLY TO ROOM TEMPERATURE, EXCEPT IN THE CASE OF FROSTBITE WHEN THAWING SHOULD ONLY BE ATTEMPTED BY MEDICAL PERSONNEL. TREAT INJURIES AND EVACUATE TO MEDIC OR TROOP MEDICAL CLINIC.	E UNLIKELY	II CRITICAL	LOW
2. EYE/HEARING LOSS	D REMOTE	II CRITICAL	MEDIUM	**RANGE OIC OR SAFETY OFFICER WILL:** 1. BRIEF STUDENTS ON THE DANGERS OF LOW HANGING BRANCHES. 2. ENSURE QUALIFICATION COURSE DETAIL PERSONNEL WEAR SAFETY GOGGLES OR GLASSES WHILE STUDENTS ARE NEGOTIATING THE COURSE. 3. BRIEF SOLDIERS ON THE DANGER OF WATCHING A LIVE GRENADE AFTER THROWING. 4. ENSURE SOLDIERS ARE WEARING HEARING PROTECTION WHEN APPROPRIATE. 5. ENSURE EXTRA EARPLUGS ARE AVAILABLE.	E UNLIKELY	II CRITICAL	LOW

FB Form 46-R, 20 Apr 95

Figure B-3. Example of risk management worksheet (continued).

RISK MANAGEMENT WORKSHEET
CONTINUATION

Operation/Training Event: MALONE 1 (HAND GRENADES)
Organization: A CO, 2/29th IN REGT
Date: RECURRING EVENT

Page 4 of 9
Prepared by: SFC ROGERS

HAZARD	INITIAL PROBABILITY	INITIAL EFFECT	INITIAL RISK LEVEL	CONTROLS IMPLEMENTED	RESIDUAL PROBABILITY	RESIDUAL EFFECT	RESIDUAL RISK LEVEL
3. SOLDIER STRUCK BY LIGHTNING	E UNLIKELY	I CATASTROPHIC	MEDIUM	RANGE OIC OR SAFETY OFFICER WILL: 1. SUSPEND ALL TRAINING DURING ELECTRICAL STORMS. 2. NOTIFY RANGE CONTROL, BATTALION HEADQUARTERS (HQ) AND COMPANY HQ OF ANY INCIDENT. 3. CONTROL THE STUDENTS. 4. BRIEF STUDENTS ON ELECTRICAL STORM PLAN AND POINT OUT LOCATION TO GROUND GEAR AND AN OPEN AREA TO MOVE TO IN THE EVENT OF LIGHTNING. INSTRUCTORS WILL: 1. ENSURE ALL STUDENTS GROUND THEIR INDIVIDUAL EQUIPMENT AND DON THEIR WET WEATHER GEAR. 2. ENSURE ALL STUDENTS ARE SPREAD 5 TO 10 METERS APART IN AN OPEN AREA, UNTIL THE STORM CLEARS OR THE TRAINING UNIT DEPARTS.	E UNLIKELY	II CRITICAL	LOW
4. SOLDIER BITTEN/STUNG BY SNAKES OR INSECTS	D REMOTE	I CATASTROPHIC	HIGH	RANGE OIC OR SAFETY OFFICER WILL: DURING A SAFETY BRIEFING, INFORM THE STUDENTS OF THE VARIOUS TYPES OF WILDLIFE THAT ARE HAZARDOUS AND WARN THEM NOT TO HANDLE OR HARASS THE WILDLIFE DURING TRAINING.	E UNLIKELY	II CRITICAL	LOW
5. FALLS	D REMOTE	II CRITICAL	MEDIUM	OIC OR SAFETY OFFICER WILL: 1. GIVE SAFETY BRIEFING ALERTING SOLDIERS TO TRIPPING HAZARDS: ROCKS, BRANCHES, FALLEN TREES, AND CREEK BEDS. 2. BRIEF SOLDIERS PRIOR TO THE HAND GRENADE QUALIFICATION COURSE (HGQC) ON SPECIFIC HAZARDS ASSOCIATED WITH THEIR RESPECTIVE COURSE.	E UNLIKELY	II CRITICAL	LOW
6. DEMONSTRATION OF AN M14 INCENDIARY GRENADE COULD BURN RETINA IN EYES	D REMOTE	II CRITICAL	MEDIUM	RSO WILL: BRIEF SOLDIERS NOT TO LOOK DIRECTLY AT THE GRENADE DURING DEMONSTRATION. INSTRUCTORS WILL: MONITOR SOLDIERS TO ENSURE THEY DO NOT LOOK AT THE GRENADE.	E UNLIKELY	III MARGINAL	LOW

FB Form 46-R, 20 Apr 95

Figure B-3. Example of risk management worksheet (continued).

RISK MANAGEMENT WORKSHEET
CONTINUATION

Operation/Training Event: MALONE 1 (HAND GRENADES)
Organization: A CO, 2/29th IN REG'T
Date: RECURRING EVENT
Prepared by: SFC ROGERS

HAZARD	INITIAL PROBABILITY	INITIAL EFFECT	INITIAL RISK LEVEL	CONTROLS IMPLEMENTED	RESIDUAL PROBABILITY	RESIDUAL EFFECT	RESIDUAL RISK LEVEL
7. SOLDIER MISSES BUNKER WHILE USING COOK OFF TECHNIQUE—FUSE RESIDUE FROM PRACTICE FUSE COULD HIT SOLDIER.	D REMOTE	III MARGINAL	LOW	**INSTRUCTORS WILL:** 1. MONITOR SOLDIERS TO ENSURE THEY DO NOT LOOK AT THE GRENADE. 2. DEMONSTRATE COOK OFF TECHNIQUES AND TALK SOLDIERS THROUGH THE TECHNIQUES. 3. ENSURE COOK OFF IS ONLY USED WITH PRACTICE FUSES. 4. ENSURE SOLDIERS TURN AND FACE THE REAR OF THE BUNKER TO KEEP FRAGMENTS FROM HITTING THEM IN THE FACE. **RANGE OIC OR SAFETY OFFICER WILL:** 1. BRIEF ALL INSTRUCTORS ON THE SAFETY PROCEDURES TO BE FOLLOWED ON THE HGQC. 2. ENSURE SOLDIERS ON DETAIL ARE WEARING EYE PROTECTION AND BLACK GLOVES WHILE RETRIEVING GRENADES. 3. ENSURE SOLDIERS ON DETAIL ARE NOT RETRIEVING GRENADES UNLESS INFORMED BY THE GRADER AND ARE NOT THROWING GRENADES AT ANY TIME.	D REMOTE	IV NEGLIGIBLE	LOW
8. BURNING HANDS ON EXPENDED PRACTICE GRENADES	D REMOTE	III MARGINAL	LOW	AMMUNITION NCO ENSURES SOLDIERS USE BLACK LEATHER SHELLS WHEN REFUSING PRACTICE FUSE HEADS.	D REMOTE	IV NEGLIGIBLE	LOW
9. AMMUNITION/ PYROTECHNICS	D REMOTE	II CRITICAL	MEDIUM	**RSO WILL:** ENSURE ALL WEAPONS HAVE BLANK ADAPTERS. **AMMUNITION NCO:** WILL KEEP ALL M67 HAND GRENADES IN THE AMMUNITION BUNKER AND UNDER GUARD AT ALL TIMES.	E UNLIKELY	II CRITICAL	LOW

FB Form 46-R, 20 Apr 95

Figure B-3. Example of risk management worksheet (continued).

RISK MANAGEMENT WORKSHEET
CONTINUATION

Operation/Training Event: MALONE 1 (HAND GRENADES)
Organization: A CO, 2/29th IN REGT

Date: RECURRING EVENT

Page 6 of 9
Prepared by: SFC ROGERS

HAZARD	INITIAL PROBABILITY	INITIAL EFFECT	INITIAL RISK LEVEL	CONTROLS IMPLEMENTED	RESIDUAL PROBABILITY	RESIDUAL EFFECT	RESIDUAL RISK LEVEL
10. SOLDIER HIT BY THROWN PRACTICE GRENADE	D REMOTE	III MARGINAL	MEDIUM	**RSO WILL:** WARN SOLDIERS TO WATCH FOR OTHER SOLDIERS IN THE PATH OF FLYING PRACTICE GRENADES AND ACTIONS TO TAKE IF IN THE PATH OF A THROWN PRACTICE GRENADE. **INSTRUCTORS WILL:** 1. ALLOW ENOUGH DISTANCE BETWEEN QUALIFYING SOLDIERS TO ENSURE OVERTHROWN PRACTICE GRENADES WILL NOT HIT SOLDIERS. 2. ENSURE SOLDIERS WEAR KEVLAR HELMET AT ALL TIMES WHILE ON, OR IN THE VICINITY OF, THE QUALIFICATION COURSE. 3. ENSURE SOLDIERS NOT INVOLVED IN THE HGQC STAY CLEAR OF THE QUALIFICATION COURSE.	E UNLIKELY	III MARGINAL	LOW
11. LOST SOLDIER	D REMOTE	II CRITICAL	MEDIUM	1. SAFETY BRIEFING WILL INCLUDE MEASURES TO TAKE IF LOST OR SEPARATED. 2. A SITUATION REPORT WILL BE PROVIDED TO THE CHAIN OF COMMAND, BN, REGT, AND RANGE CONTROL. 3. A THOROUGH SEARCH WILL BE CONDUCTED FOR THE LOST SOLDIER IN COORDINATION WITH TRAINING COMPANY CADRE AND USING ALL AVAILABLE MANPOWER.	E UNLIKELY	III MARGINAL	LOW
12. ROAD CONDITIONS	D REMOTE	II CRITICAL	MEDIUM	1. RSO GIVES DETAILED SAFETY BRIEFING. 2. 5 M.P.H. SPEED LIMIT SIGNS ARE POSTED IN THE TRAINING AREA. 3. SAFETY BRIEFING INCLUDES CURRENT AND EXPECTED WEATHER CONDITIONS AND THE POSSIBLE EFFECT ON ROAD CONDITIONS.	D REMOTE	III MARGINAL	LOW

FB Form 46-R, 20 Apr 95

RISK MANAGEMENT WORKSHEET
CONTINUATION

Operation/Training Event: MALONE 1 (HAND GRENADES)
Organization: A CO, 2/29th IN REGT
Date: RECURRING EVENT
Prepared by: SFC ROGERS

HAZARD	INITIAL PROBABILITY	INITIAL EFFECT	INITIAL RISK LEVEL	CONTROLS IMPLEMENTED	RESIDUAL PROBABILITY	RESIDUAL EFFECT	RESIDUAL RISK LEVEL
13. MANDATORY TRAINING PRIOR TO LIVE BAY	D REMOTE	III MARGINAL	MEDIUM	1. SOLDIERS ARE TAUGHT PROPER GRIP AND THROWING TECHNIQUE AT "DISTANCE AND ACCURACY" TRAINING AND THE TRAINING IS REINFORCED IN THE MOCK BAY. 2. ALL SOLDIERS MUST SUCCESSFULLY COMPLETE "DISTANCE AND ACCURACY" AND MOCK BAY TRAINING PRIOR TO ENTERING THE LIVE BAY.	E UNLIKELY	II CRITICAL	LOW
14. RANGE SPECIFIC HAZARDS				3. AT THE MOCK BAY SOLDIERS RECEIVE DEMONSTRATIONS AND REHEARSE THE EVACUATION DRILL AS STATED UNDER "RANGE SPECIFIC HAZARDS". 4. ALL INSTRUCTORS WILL REHEARSE AND ALL UNASSIGNED INSTRUCTORS WILL BE RECERTIFIED ON THE PIT EVACUATION DRILLS THE MORNING PRIOR TO CONDUCTING A LIVE BAY EXERCISE. PRIMARY INSTRUCTOR (PI) WILL CONTROL INSTRUCTOR ROTATION ENSURING A 10 MINUTE BREAK EVERY 30 MINUTES. 5. THE PIT NCO WILL BE A SSG CERTIFIED BY THE RANGE OIC AND A/2-29 COMPANY COMMANDER. 6. TRAINING COMPANY COMMANDER OR FIRST SERGEANT WILL BE ON SITE DURING LIVE GRENADE THROW IAW TRAINING BRIGADE POLICY.			
14(A). ARMED HAND GRENADE DROPPED IN LIVE BAY	D REMOTE	I CATASTROPHIC	HIGH	PIT NCO WILL DIRECT AND CONTROL THE SOLDIER HE HAS IN THE PIT WITH HIM AND MAINTAIN POSITIVE VISUAL OBSERVATION AND CONTROL OF THE LIVE GRENADES THE ENTIRE TIME THE SOLDIER IS IN THE PIT.	E UNLIKELY	I CATASTROPHIC	MEDIUM
14(B). HAND GRENADE DROPPED OFF BACK WALL	C OCCASIONAL	II CRITICAL	HIGH	PIT NCO AND SOLDIER EXECUTE THE EVACUATION DRILL, AS REHEARSED IN THE MOCK BAY. EXITING THE PIT OVER THE BACK WALL. PIT NCO WILL ENSURE, PHYSICALLY IF NECESSARY, THE SOLDIER GETS OVER THE BACK WALL.	D REMOTE	II CRITICAL	MEDIUM
14(C). SOLDIER WATCHES GRENADE AFTER THROW	C OCCASIONAL	II CRITICAL	HIGH	PIT NCO AND SOLDIER EXECUTE SAFETY DRILL, AS REHEARSED IN THE MOCK BAY. PIT NCO AND SOLDIER WILL ASSUME THE PRONE POSITION PARALLEL TO THE BACK WALL. PIT NCO WILL ENSURE THE SOLDIER'S HEAD IS BELOW THE TOP OF THE BACK WALL. PIT NCO WILL PHYSICALLY PULL THE SOLDIER DOWN BEHIND THE FRONT WALL OF THE LIVE BAY.	D REMOTE	II CRITICAL	MEDIUM

FB Form 46-R, 20 Apr 95

Figure B-3. Example of risk management worksheet (continued).

Figure B-3. Example of risk management worksheet (continued).

RISK MANAGEMENT WORKSHEET
CONTINUATION

Operation/Training Event: MALONE 1 (HAND GRENADES)   Page 8 of 9
Organization: A CO, 2/29th IN REGT
Date: RECURRING EVENT   Prepared by: SFC ROGERS

HAZARD	INITIAL PROBABILITY	INITIAL EFFECT	INITIAL RISK LEVEL	CONTROLS IMPLEMENTED	RESIDUAL PROBABILITY	RESIDUAL EFFECT	RESIDUAL RISK LEVEL
14(D), SOLDIER FREEZES AFTER ARMING GRENADE	D REMOTE	II CRITICAL	MEDIUM	PIT NCO WILL REINFORCE THE COMMAND "THROW GRENADE." PIT NCO WILL GRASP SOLDIER'S HAND AND APPLY PRESSURE TO THE SAFETY LEVER. PIT NCO WILL WALK SOLDIER FORWARD AND EXTEND HIS HANDS OVER THE FRONT WALL. PIT NCO ENSURES SOLDIER'S HEAD IS BELOW THE FRONT WALL, THEN LETS THE SOLDIER DROP THE GRENADE IN FRONT OF THE LIVE BAY.	E UNLIKELY	II CRITICAL	LOW
14(E), SOLDIER COOKS OFF GRENADE	C OCCASIONAL	I CATASTROPHIC	HIGH	PIT NCO CONTINUES TO REINFORCE THE COMMAND TO "THROW GRENADE." PIT NCO WILL NOT ATTEMPT TO GRAB THE GRENADE DUE TO THE RISK THAT SOLDIER MAY DROP IT IN THE LIVE BAY.	D REMOTE	I CATASTROPHIC	HIGH
14(F), SOLDIER MILKS GRENADE PRIOR TO THROWING	C OCCASIONAL	I CATASTROPHIC	HIGH	IF PIT NCO HEARS METALLIC CLICK (GRENADE ARMED), HE WILL REINFORCE THE COMMAND "THROW GRENADE." IF PIT NCO DOES NOT HEAR A METALLIC CLICK (GRENADE NOT ARMED), HE WILL GRAB THE SOLDIER'S HAND AND APPLY PRESSURE TO THE SAFETY LEVER. PIT NCO WILL WALK THE SOLDIER TO THE FRONT WALL, ENSURE SOLDIER'S HEAD IS BELOW THE FRONT WALL, AND LET THE SOLDIER DROP THE GRENADE IN FRONT OF THE LIVE BAY.	D REMOTE	I CATASTROPHIC	HIGH
14(G), SOLDIERS BEING HIT BY FRAGMENTS FROM THE M67 FRAGMENTATION GRENADE	D REMOTE	II CRITICAL	MEDIUM	1. RSO ENSURES ALL SOLDIERS ARE WEARING KEVLAR VESTS WHILE FORWARD OF THE SAFETY BARRIER AND WHILE THROWING THE LIVE M67 FRAGMENTATION GRENADE. 2. OIC ENSURES MEDIC WITH AID BAG IS IN THE TOWER DURING LIVE GRENADE TRAINING, AND THE AMBULANCE IS NEXT TO RANGE SHACK. 3. PI/DRILL SERGEANTS (DSs) ENSURE KEVLAR HELMET IS WORN AT ALL TIMES. 4. SOLDIERS WILL BE UNDER OVERHEAD COVER AT ALL TIMES EXCEPT WHEN THEY THEMSELVES ARE THROWING THEIR HAND GRENADES. 5. DSs/INSTRUCTORS WILL CONTROL SOLDIERS UNDER OVERHEAD COVER.	E UNLIKELY		

FB Form 46-R, 20 Apr 95

RISK MANAGEMENT WORKSHEET
CONTINUATION

Operation/Training Event: MALONE 1 (HAND GRENADES)
Organization: A CO, 2/29th IN REG'T

Date: RECURRING EVENT

Prepared by: SFC ROGERS

Page 9 of 9

HAZARD	INITIAL PROBABILITY	INITIAL EFFECT	INITIAL RISK LEVEL	CONTROLS IMPLEMENTED	RESIDUAL PROBABILITY	RESIDUAL EFFECT	RESIDUAL RISK LEVEL
14(f). HEARING LOSS FROM EXPLOSION	B LIKELY	III MARGINAL	MEDIUM	1. DSs ENSURE SOLDIERS ARE WEARING HEARING PROTECTION AT ALL TIMES WHILE AT LIVE BAY. 2. PL ENSURES EXTRA EAR PLUGS ARE AVAILABLE	D REMOTE	F NEGLIGIBLE	LOW
14(f). PREMATURE DETONATION AT GRENADE ISSUE POINT	D REMOTE	I CATASTROPHIC	HIGH	1. AMMUNITION NCO MAINTAINS NO MORE THAN TWO CASES (60 GRENADES) AT THE ISSUE POINT AT ANY ONE TIME. 2. AMMUNITION NCO ISSUES M67 FRAGMENTATION GRENADES DIRECTLY FROM CANISTER TO THE SOLDIER	E UNLIKELY	I CATASTROPHIC	MEDIUM

FB Form 46-R, 20 Apr 95

Figure B-3. Example of risk management worksheet (continued).

RANGE CONSTRUCTION/MODIFICATION

This appendix provides structural dimensions and safety requirements for the construction and modification of a hand grenade range.

C-1. STRUCTURAL DIMENSIONS

The structural dimensions of live-bay throwing pits are accomplished IAW Chapter 4 with a separation distance of 25 meters between each lane. This places adjacent pits outside the effective casualty-producing radius of 15 meters for the M67 fragmentation grenade. A rear wall (knee wall) is constructed no more than 0.6 meter (2 feet) high and 0.15 meter (6 inches) thick. It extends the width of the throwing pit, connecting both ends of the enclosure. Slope the top of the knee wall inward to allow any grenade dropped on the wall to roll into the throwing pit. Install drain pipes (no more than 2 inches in diameter) in the knee wall to allow throwing pit drainage. Slope the floor of the pits in the direction of the drainage pipes. Do not construct grenade sumps or ditches inside the throwing pits (Figure C-1).

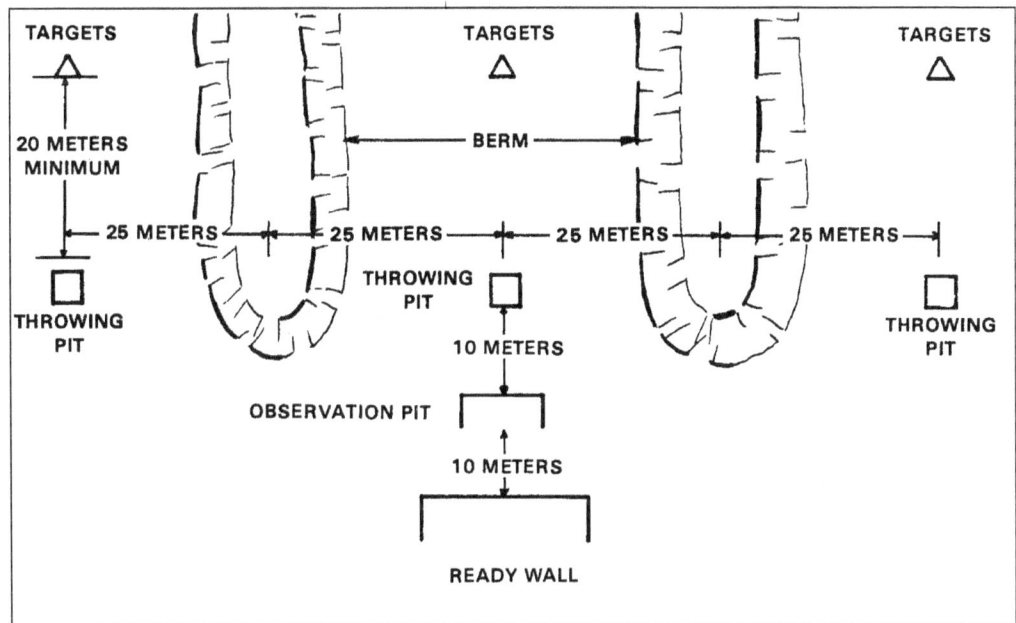

Figure C-1. Range layout.

C-2. SAND/SAWDUST PIT AND THROWING PIT

A sand/sawdust pit is placed outside the knee wall to cushion the fall of personnel diving over the wall in the event a grenade is dropped in the throwing pit (Figure C-2).

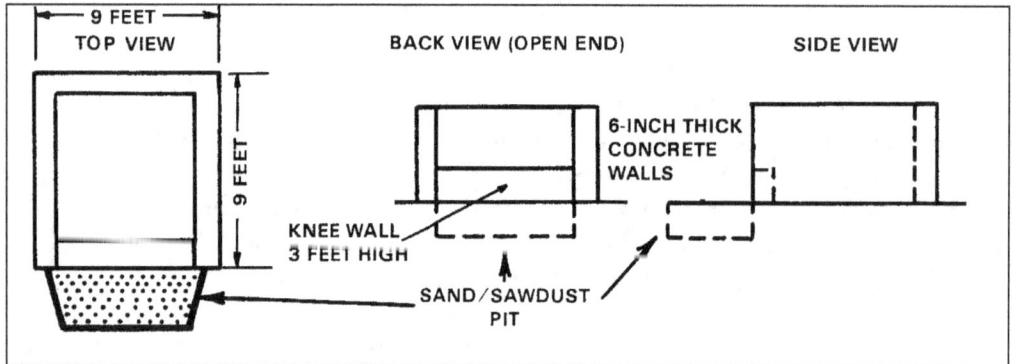

Figure C-2. Sand/sawdust pit and throwing pit.

C-3. PIT SEPARATIONS

Where possible, separate the throwing pits by using steel, concrete, or wooden revetments or earthen berms of a length and height to lessen the effect of high velocity, low angle fragments (for example, 50 meters long and 1.8 meters high). The thickness varies according to the type of construction used. This permits grenade throwing to continue from the adjacent pit when a dud grenade requires closure of a specific pit pending dud disposal.

C-4. OBSERVATION PITS

Observation pits are built of a sufficient height to enable the OIC to observe and control all throwing pits. Laminated windowpanes, constructed as described below, provide the necessary degree of safety for the observation pits.

- 10-mm glass (outside).
- 7-mm polycarbonate resin sheet.
- 6-mm glass.
- 6-mm polycarbonate resin sheet.
- 6-mm glass.

Total: 35 mm (about 1 3/8 inches).

THREAT HAND GRENADES

This appendix provides general information on common threat hand grenade identification, functions, and capabilities. North Korea, China, and many former Soviet Union nations have an extensive inventory of hand grenades. As with most equipment in use by these nations, older hand grenades remain in circulation and use long after being classified obsolete.

Section I. FORMER SOVIET UNION NATIONS

D-1. RGN OFFENSIVE HAND GRENADE
- Type: Offensive. (Figure D-1)
- Weight: 310 grams.
- Body Material: Aluminum.
- Filler Material: 114 grams A-1X-1 (RDX 96 percent, wax 4 percent) explosive.
- Fuze Type: Striker release, impact, or self-destruct.
- Fuze Delay: Impact, 1 to 2 seconds; time, 3.5 to 4 seconds (self-destruct).
- Range Thrown: 30 meters.
- Lethal Radius: 4 meters.

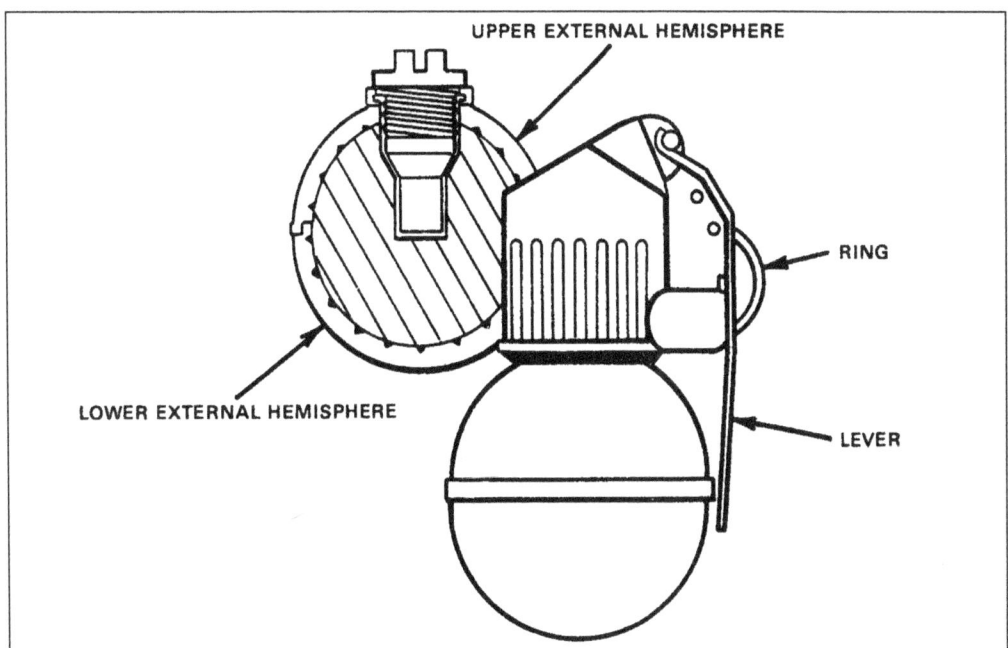

Figure D-1. RGN hand grenade.

D-2. RGO DEFENSIVE HAND GRENADE
- Type: Defensive. (Figure D-2)
- Weight: 530 grams.
- Body Material: Aluminum.
- Filler Material: 92 grams A-1X-1 (RDX 96 percent, wax 4 percent) explosive.
- Fuze Type: Striker release, impact, or self-destruct.
- Fuze Delay: Impact, 1 to 2 seconds; time, 3.5 to 4 seconds.
- Range Thrown: 30 to 40 meters.
- Lethal Radius: 6 meters.

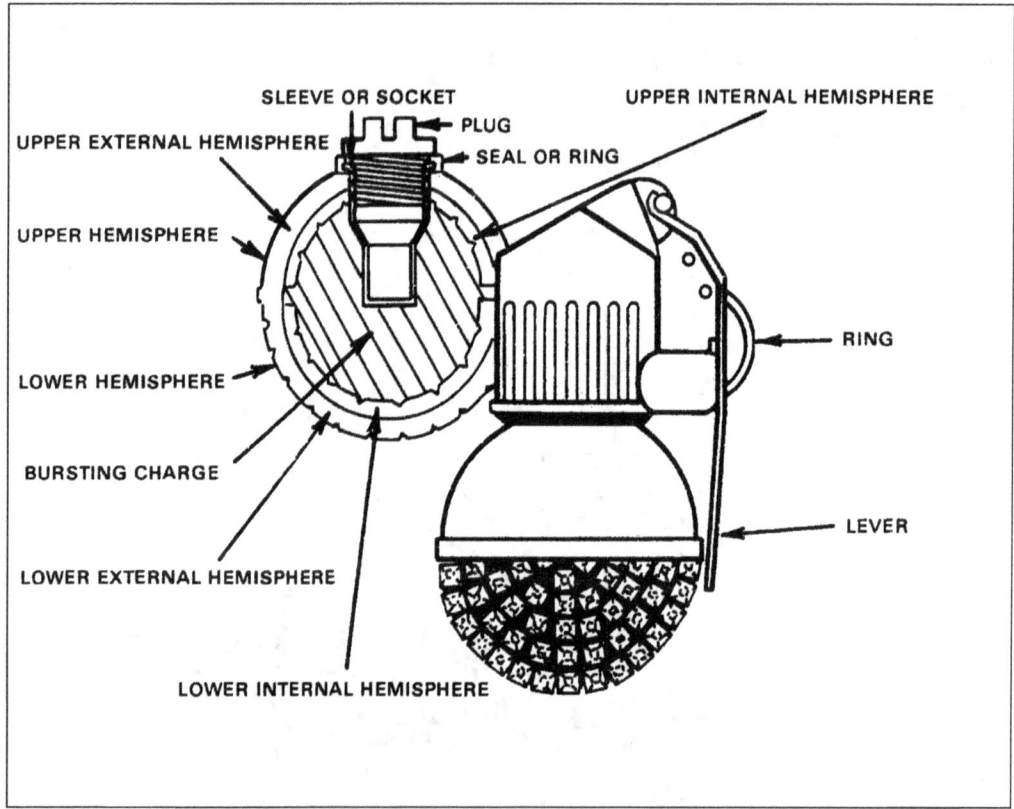

Figure D-2. RGO hand grenade.

D-3. F1 FRAGMENTATION HAND GRENADE

- Type: Fragmentation. (Figure D-3)
- Weight: 700 grams.
- Body Material: Cast iron.
- Filler Material: 60 grams TNT.
- Fuze Type: Striker release.
- Fuze Delay: 3 to 4 seconds; for booby traps, 0 to 13 seconds.
- Range Thrown: 30 meters.
- Lethal Radius: 20 to 30 meters.

NOTE: The F1 has been copied and produced by numerous other countries throughout the world.

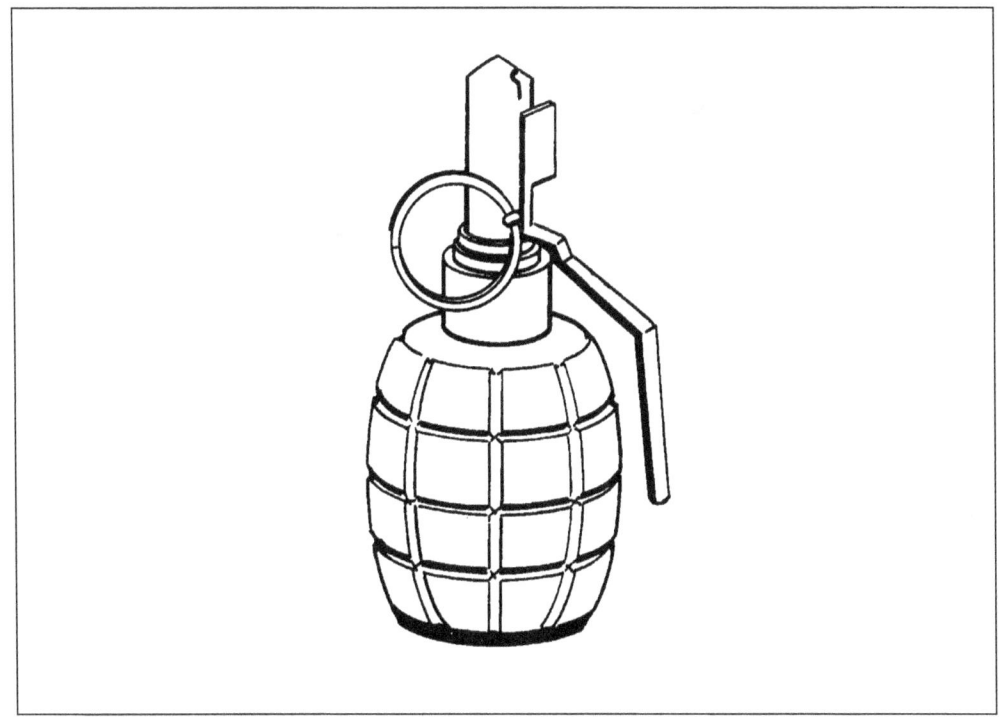

Figure D-3. F1 hand grenade.

D-4. RKG-3M ANTITANK HAND GRENADE

- Type: Antitank. (Figure D-4)
- Weight: With fuze, 1.07 kilograms.
- Weight of HE Filling: TNT/RDX, 540 grams.
- Penetration: 125 millimeters.
- Fuze Type: Instantaneous impact, base detonating.
- Effective Fragment Radius: 20 meters.
- Length: 350 millimeters.
- Diameter: 65 millimeters.

NOTE: The RKG-3 family of grenades has been copied and produced by numerous other countries throughout the world.

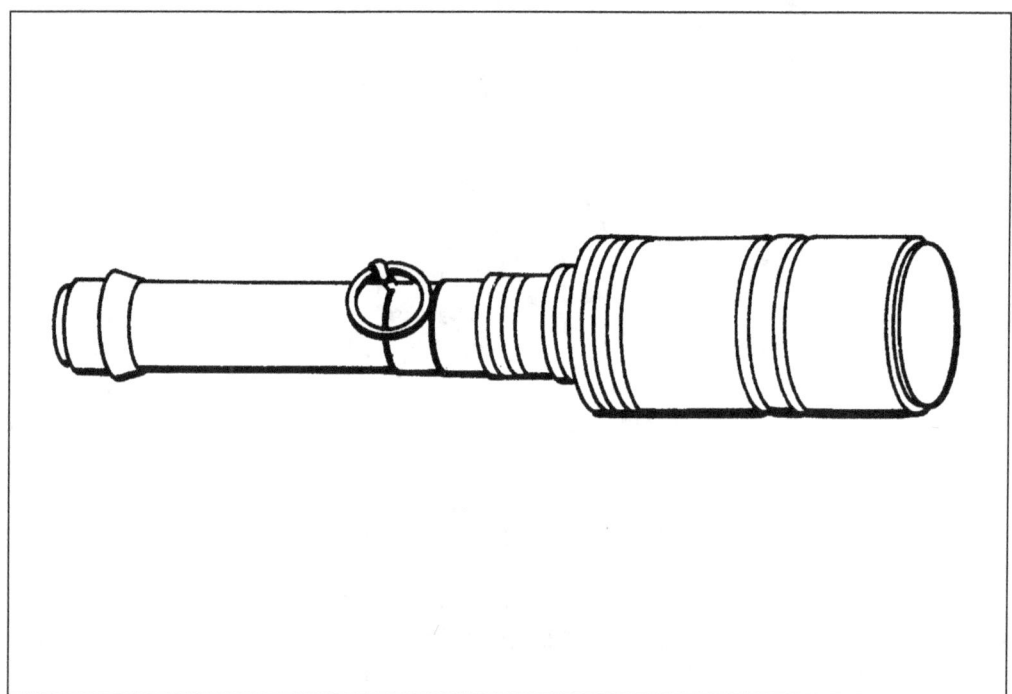

Figure D-4. RKG-3M antitank hand grenade.

D-5. RGD-5 FRAGMENTATION HAND GRENADE
- Type: Fragmentation. (Figure D-5)
- Weight: 310 grams.
- Filler Material: 110 grams of TNT.
- Fuze Delay: 3 to 4 seconds.
- Range Thrown: 40 meters.
- Effective Fragment Radius: 15 to 20 meters, maximum fragment range about 30 meters.

NOTE: The RGD-5 has been copied and produced by numerous other countries throughout the world.

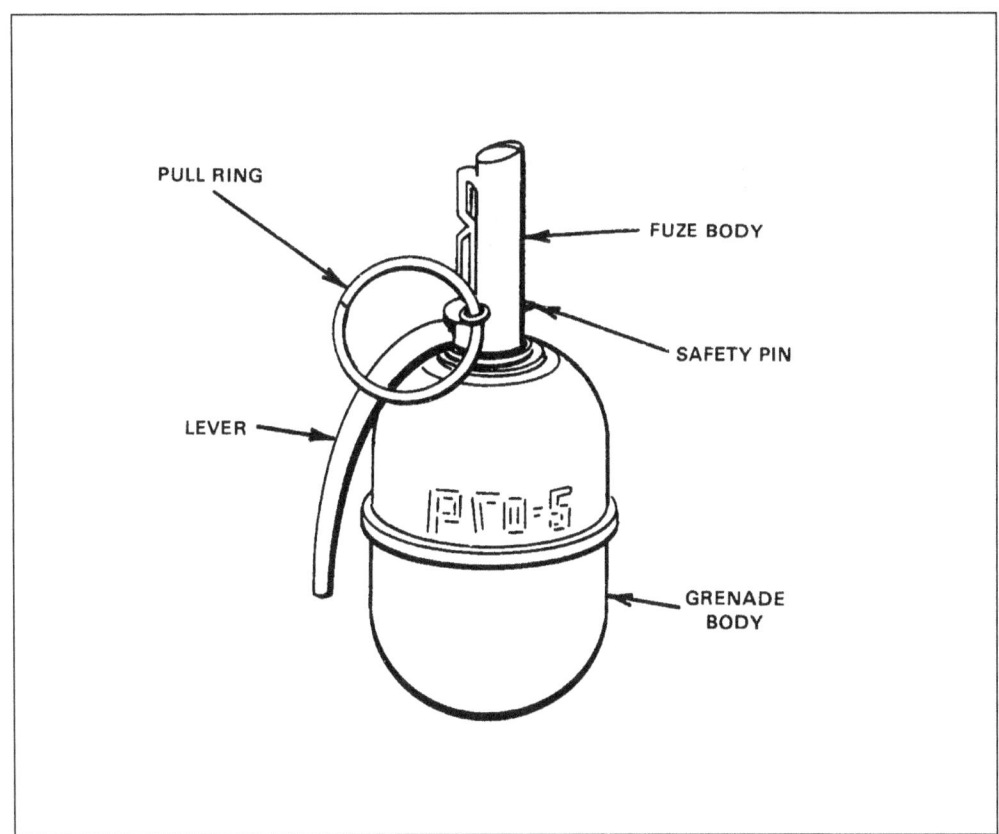

Figure D-5. RGD-5 hand grenade.

D-6. RG-42 FRAGMENTATION HAND GRENADE
- Type: Fragmentation. (Figure D-6)
- Weight: 435 grams.
- Body Material: Steel.
- Filler Material: 110 to 120 grams TNT.
- Fuze Type: Striker release.
- Fuze Delay: 3.2 to 4.2 seconds.
- Range Thrown: 30 meters.
- Effective Fragment Radius: 20 meters.

NOTE: The RG-42 has been copied and produced by numerous other countries throughout the world.

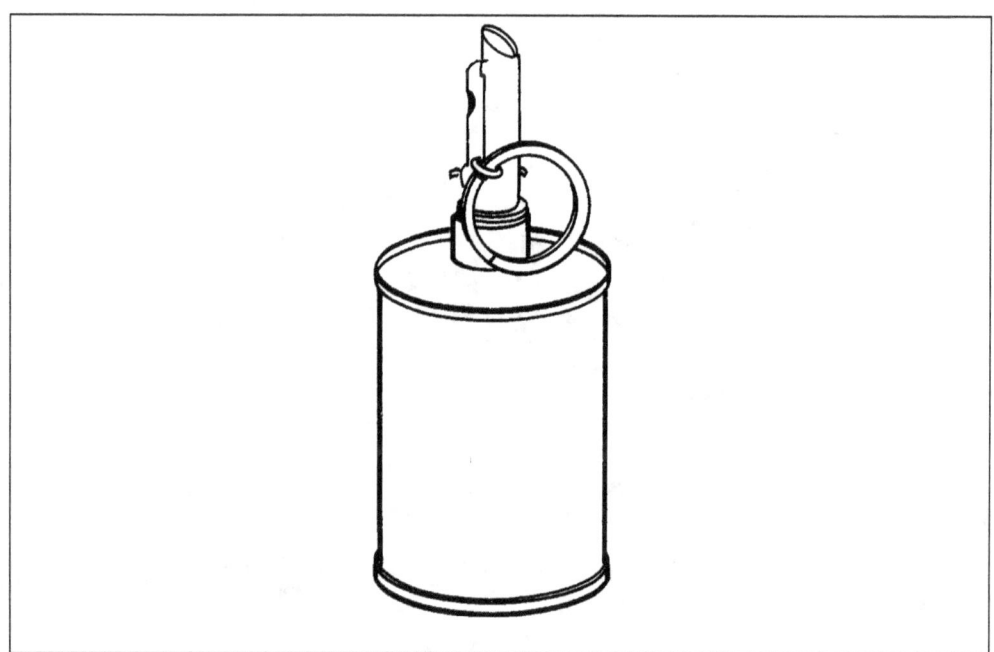

Figure D-6. RG-42 hand grenade.

D-7. RDG-1

- Type: Hand, smoke. (Figure D-7)
- Weight: 500 grams.
- Body Material: Cardboard, handle wood/cardboard.
- Burning Time: 60 to 90 seconds.
- Fuze: Friction fuze.
- Fuze Delay: Unknown.
- Filler: Smoke mixture.
- Range Thrown: 35 meters.

NOTE: This grenade is used to screen river crossings because it floats.

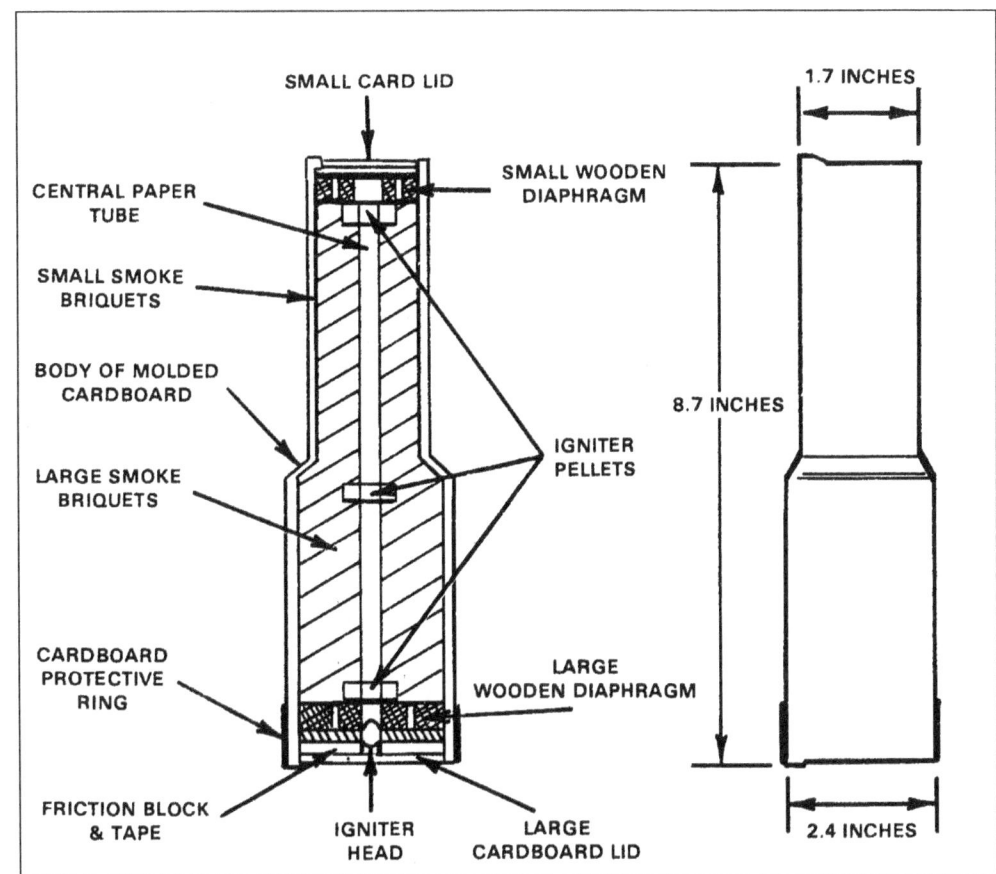

Figure D-7. RDG-1 smoke grenade.

D-8. RDG-2 AND RDG-3

- Type: Smoke. (Figure D-8)
- Weight: 500 grams.
- Body Material: Cardboard coated with wax, handle wood/cardboard.
- Burning Time: 50 to 90 seconds.
- Fuze: Friction fuze.
- Fuze Delay: Unknown.
- Filler: Smoke mixture.
- Range Thrown: 35 meters.

NOTE: This grenade does not float and is unsuitable for water use.

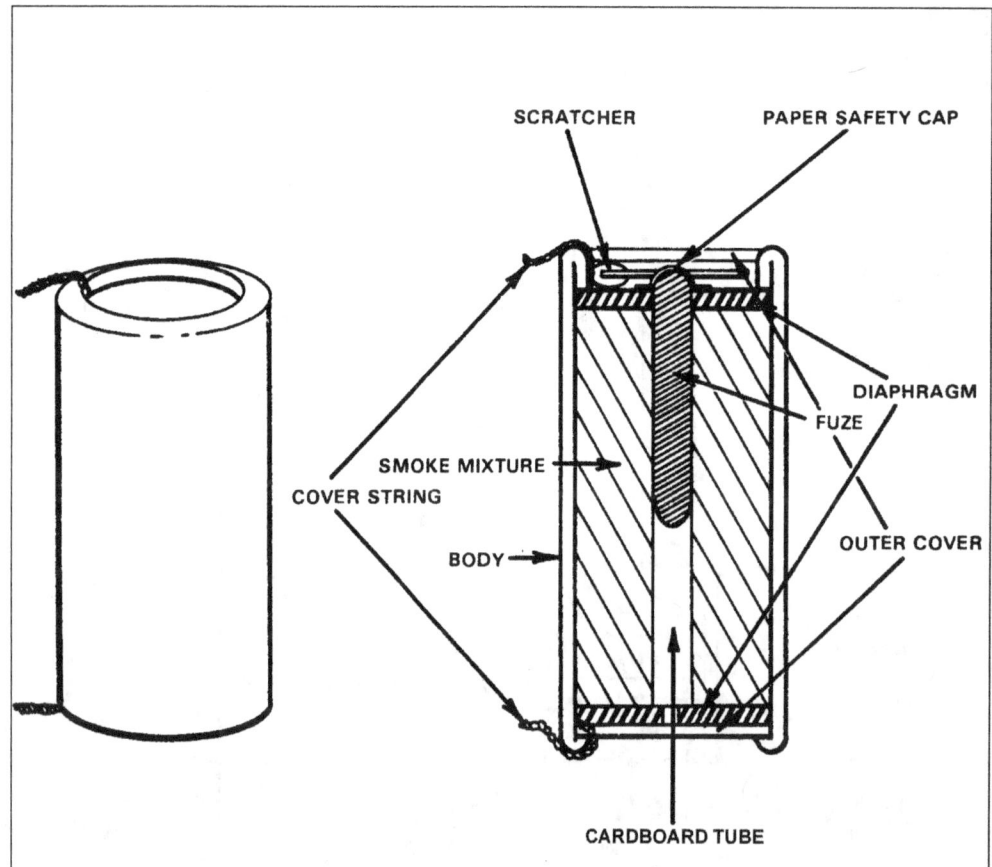

Figure D-8. RDG-2 and RDG-3 smoke grenade.

Section II. NORTH KOREA

D-9. ROUND FRAGMENTATION GRENADE

- Type: Fragmentation. (Figure D-9)
- Weight: 600 grams.
- Body Material: Cast aluminum body with 140 to 150 cast iron balls embedded in it.
- Fuze: Striker release.
- Fuze Delay: 3.2 to 4.2 seconds.
- Filler: TNT, 60 grams.
- Effective Casualty Radius: 20 meters.

NOTE: A variation of this grenade has a plastic body.

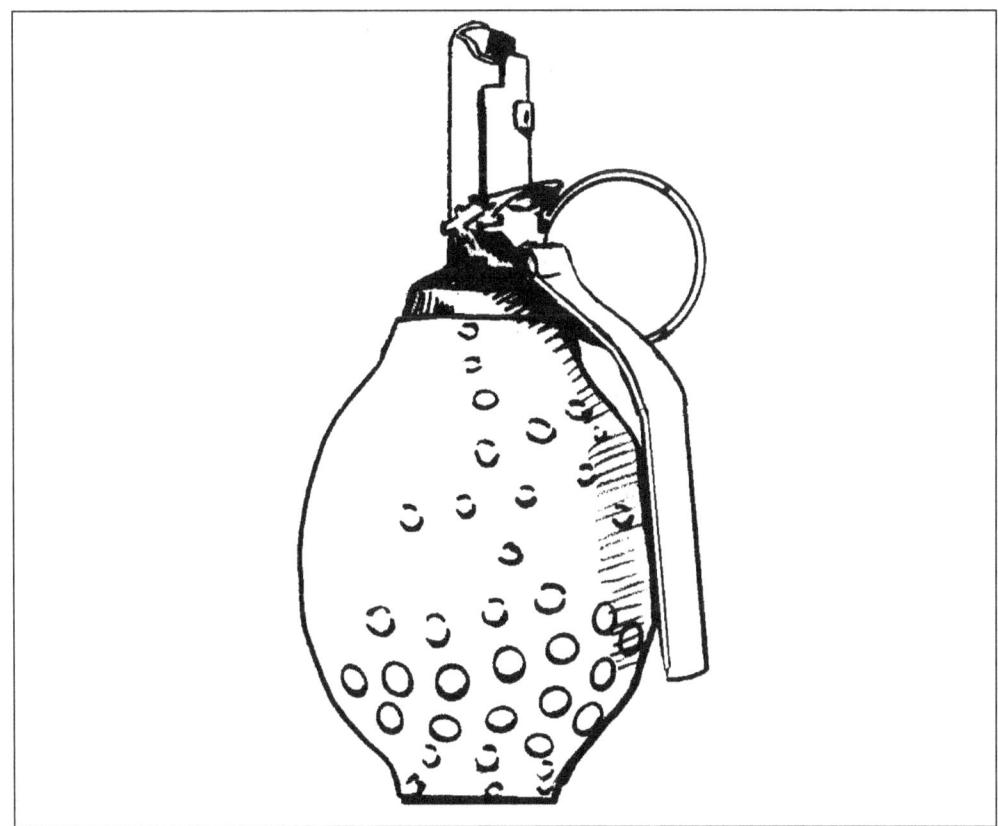

Figure D-9. North Korean fragmentation grenade (round).

D-10. RECTANGULAR FRAGMENTATION GRENADE

- Type: Fragmentation. (Figure D-10)
- Weight: 370 grams.
- Body Material: Sheet steel with about 1,300 steel balls in a cavity between the outer wall and the explosive filler.
- Fuze: Striker release.
- Fuze Delay: 3.2 to 4.2 seconds.
- Filler: Composition B, 55 grams.
- Effective Casualty Radius: 20 meters.

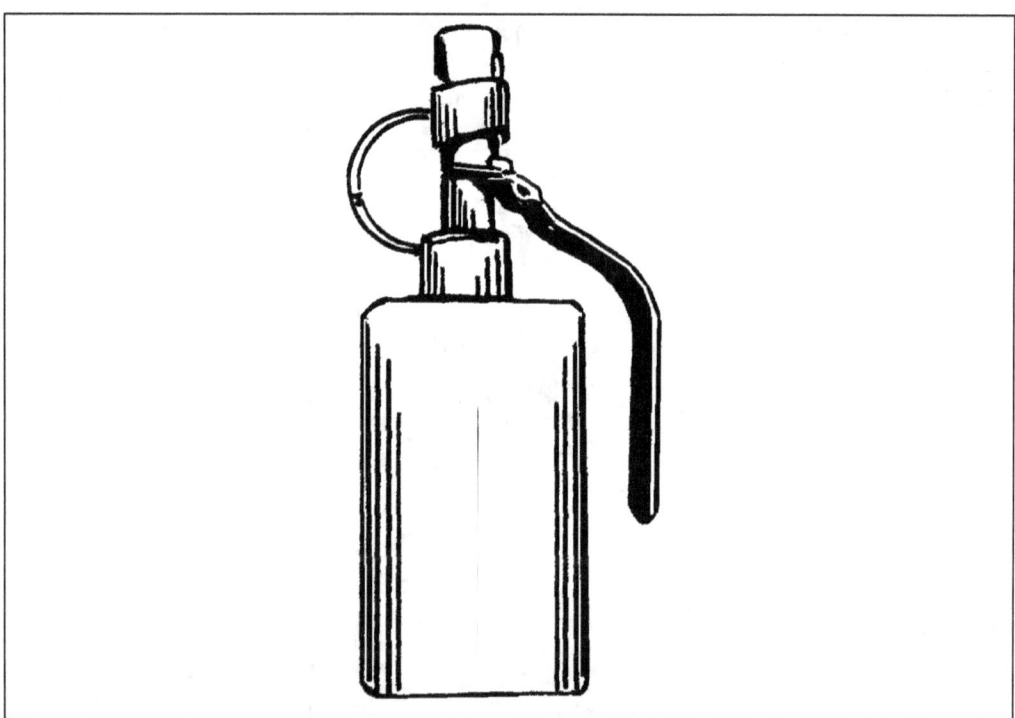

Figure D-10. North Korean fragmentation grenade (rectangular).

D-11. LACHRYMATORY GRENADE

- Type: Lachrymatory. (Figure D-11)
- Weight: 350 grams.
- Body Material: Sheet steel with a wooden handle.
- Fuze: Pull friction.
- Fuze Delay: 3 to 4 seconds.
- Filler: CS mixture/TNT.
- Range Thrown: 20 meters.
- Effective Radius: 10 meters.

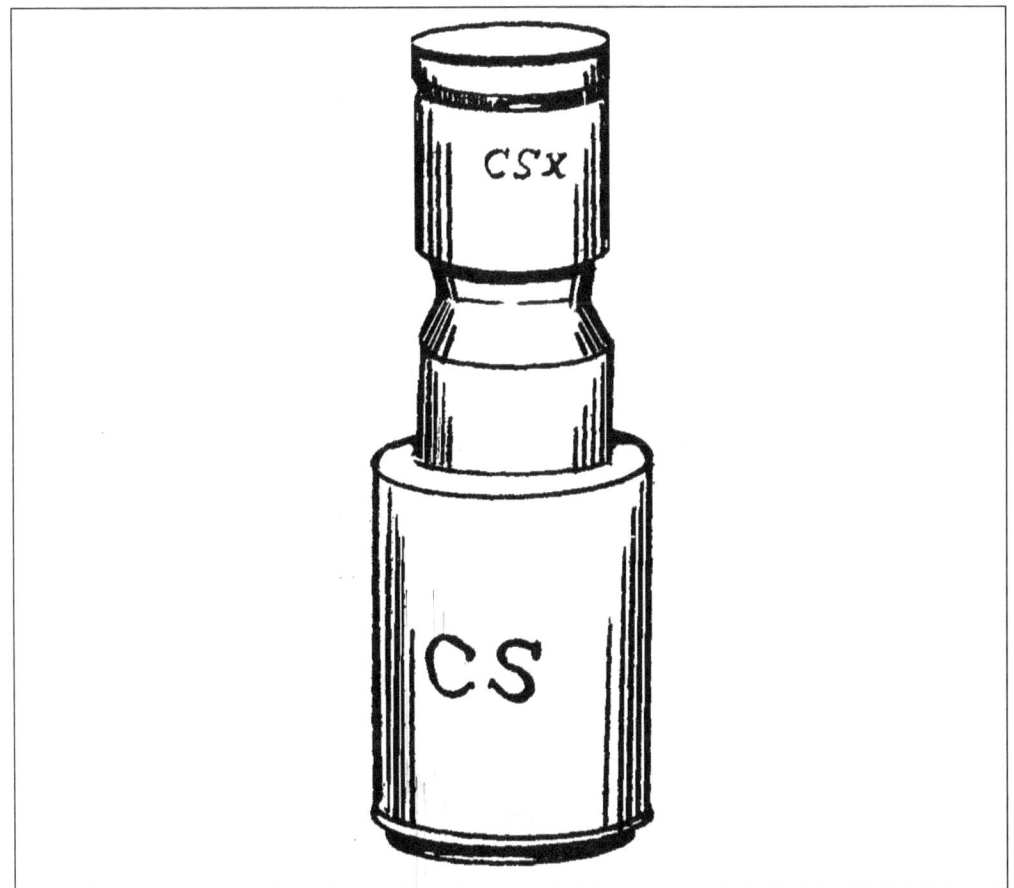

Figure D-11. North Korean lachrymatory grenade.

Section III. CHINA

D-12. TYPE 1 FRAGMENTATION GRENADE

- Type: Fragmentation. (Figure D-12)
- Weight: 600 grams.
- Body Material: Cast iron.
- Fuze: Striker release.
- Fuze Delay: 3 to 4 seconds.
- Filler: TNT, 50 grams.
- Lethal Range: 20 meters.

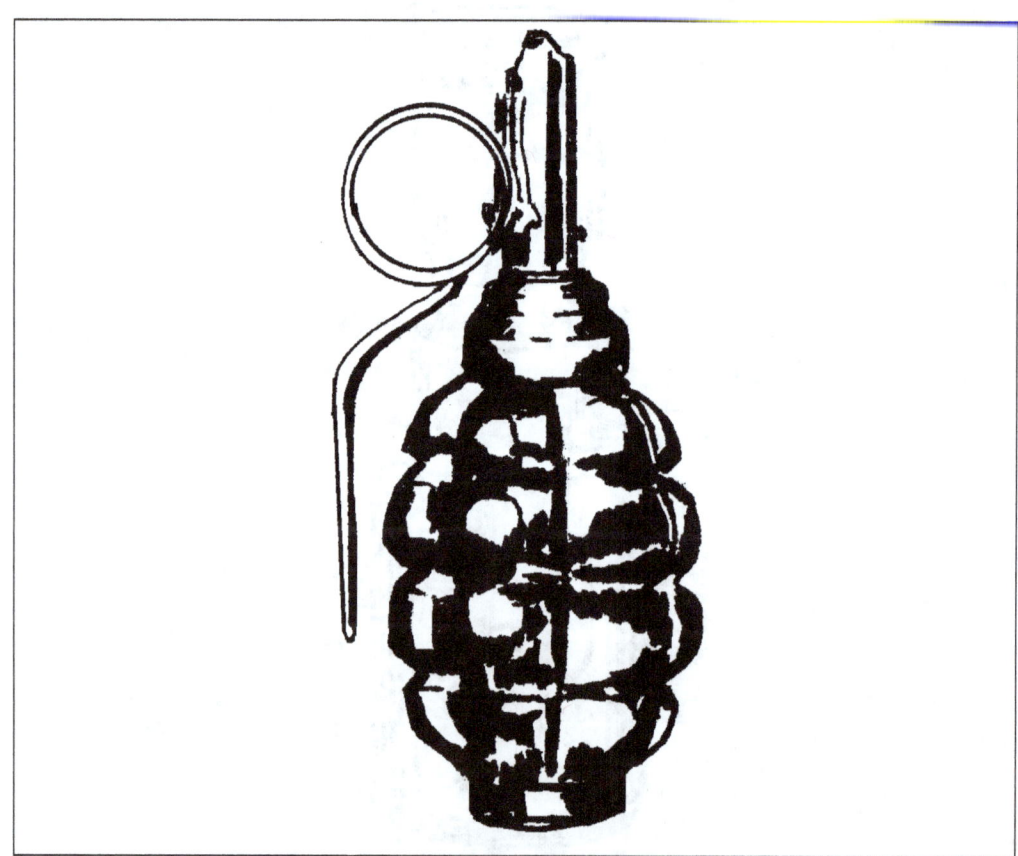

Figure D-12. Type 1 fragmentation grenade.

D-13. TYPE 73 FRAGMENTATION GRENADE

- Type: Fragmentation. (Figure D-13)
- Weight: 190 grams.
- Body Material: Two-piece sheet metal body enclosing a layer of 580 steel balls.
- Fuze: Percussion.
- Fuze Delay: 0.5 to 1 second.
- Filler: Unknown.
- Effective Casualty Radius: 7 meters.

NOTE: A variation of this grenade may be in use as a rifle grenade with a tail fin assembly.

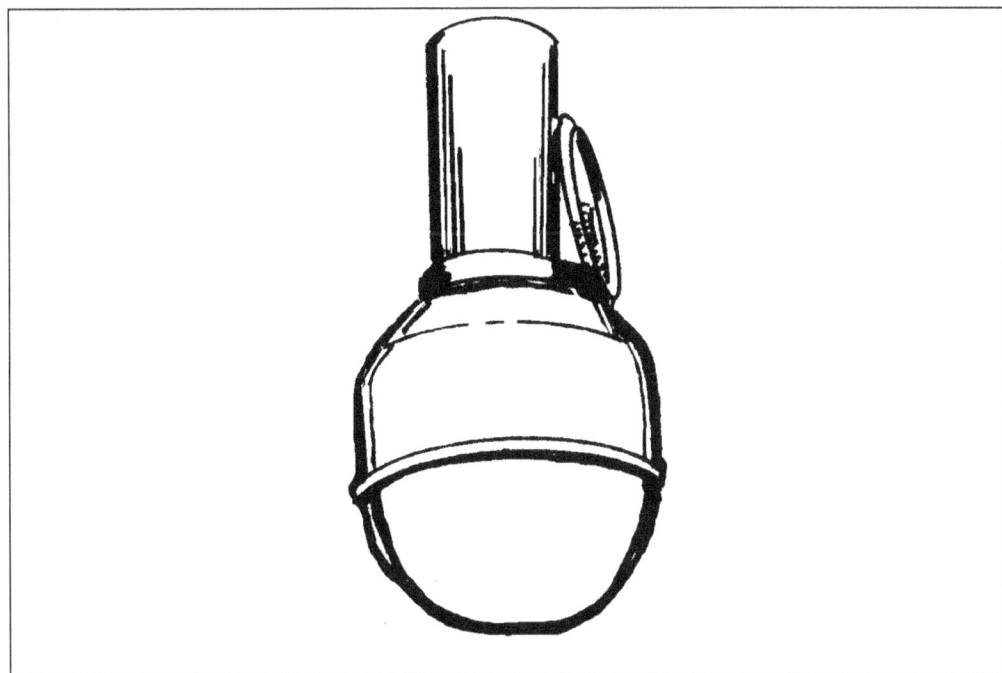

Figure D-13. Type 73 fragmentation grenade.

D-14. TYPE 77-1 FRAGMENTATION STICK

- Type: Fragmentation. (Figure D-14)
- Weight: 380 grams.
- Body Material: Cast iron with a plastic handle and sheet metal or plastic fuze cover cap.
- Fuze: Pull friction.
- Fuze Delay: 2.8 to 4 seconds.
- Filler: TNT, 70 grams.
- Lethal Radius: 7 meters.

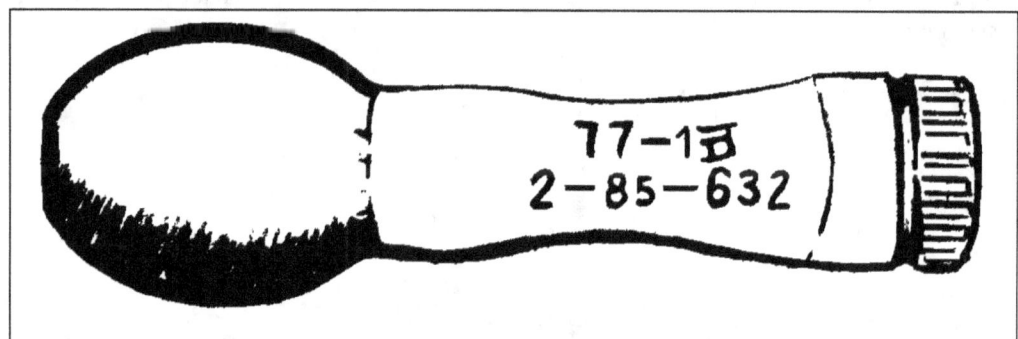

Figure D-14. Type 77-1 fragmentation stick.

D-15. SC-2 LACHRYMATORY GRENADE

- Type: Lachrymatory (explosively dispersed). (Figure D-15)
- Weight: 110 grams.
- Body Material: Plastic.
- Fuze: Striker release or friction.
- Fuze Delay: 2.8 to 3.6 seconds.
- Filler: Tear agent, 25 grams.
- Coverage: 300 cubic meters.

Figure D-15. SC-2 lachrymatory grenade.

D-16. SC-2 LACHRYMATORY/SMOKE GRENADE

- Type: Lachrymatory/smoke. (Figure D-16)
- Weight: 110 grams.
- Body Material: Plastic.
- Fuze: Striker release or friction.
- Fuze Delay: 1.8 to 2.8 seconds.
- Filler: Tear agent/smoke mixture, 70 grams.
- Coverage: 300 cubic meters.

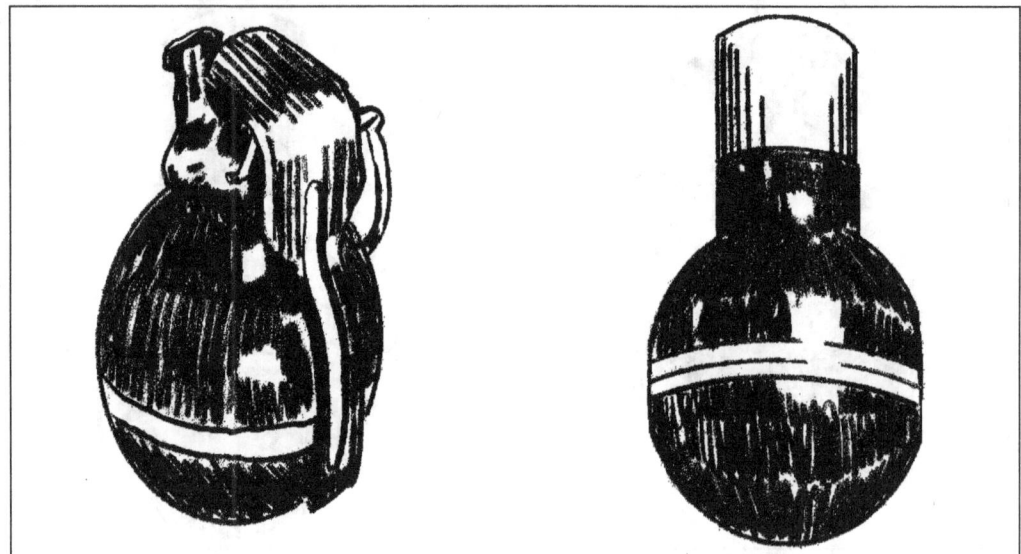

Figure D-16. SC-2 lachrymatory/smoke grenade.

D-17. JYD-1

- Type: Rubber ball. (Figure D-17)
- Weight: 150 grams.
- Body Material: Plastic.
- Fuze: Striker release or friction.
- Fuze Delay: 2.8 to 3.4 seconds.
- Filler: 840 rubber balls; bursting charge, 4 grams.
- Effective radius: 0.3 to 3 meters.

Figure D-17. JYD-1 rubber ball grenade.

D-18. JYB-1

- Type: Stun. (Figure D-18)
- Weight: 150 grams.
- Body Material: Plastic.
- Fuze: Striker release or friction.
- Fuze Delay: 3 to 4 seconds.
- Filler: Pyrotechnic mixture, 45 grams.
- Coverage: Sound level over 150 decibels within 10 meters.

Figure D-18. JYB-1 stun grenade.

D-19. JYS-1

- Type: Flash/bang. (Figure D-19)
- Weight: 45 grams.
- Body Material: Plastic.
- Fuze: Striker release or friction.
- Fuze Delay: Unknown.
- Filler: Pyrotechnic mixture, 25 grams.
- Effective Range: 10 meters.
- Flash Intensity: 40,000,000 candella.

Figure D-19. JYS-1 flash/bang grenade.

APPENDIX E
OBSOLETE HAND GRENADES

This appendix provides data for identifying and understanding the description and capabilities of obsolete US hand grenades. Although these grenades are no longer common to the US inventory, the majority of them are still in use by other services or nations.

E-1. M30 PRACTICE HAND GRENADE

The M30 practice grenade (Figure E-1) simulates the M26 series of fragmentation hand grenades for training purposes. The M30 adds realism to training and familiarizes the soldier with the functioning and description of the fragmentation hand grenade.

    a. **Body**. The grenade body is cast iron and is reusable.

    b. **Fuze**. The fuze is an M205A1 or M205A2.

    c. **Weight**. The grenade weighs 16 ounces.

    d. **Safety Clip**. See paragraph 1-3.

    e. **Capabilities**. The average soldier can throw the grenade 40 meters. The M30 emits a small puff of white smoke after a delay of 4 to 5 seconds and makes a loud popping sound.

    f. **Color and Markings**. The grenade is light blue with white markings.

WARNING
Fuze fragments can exit the hole in the base of the grenade body and cause injury.

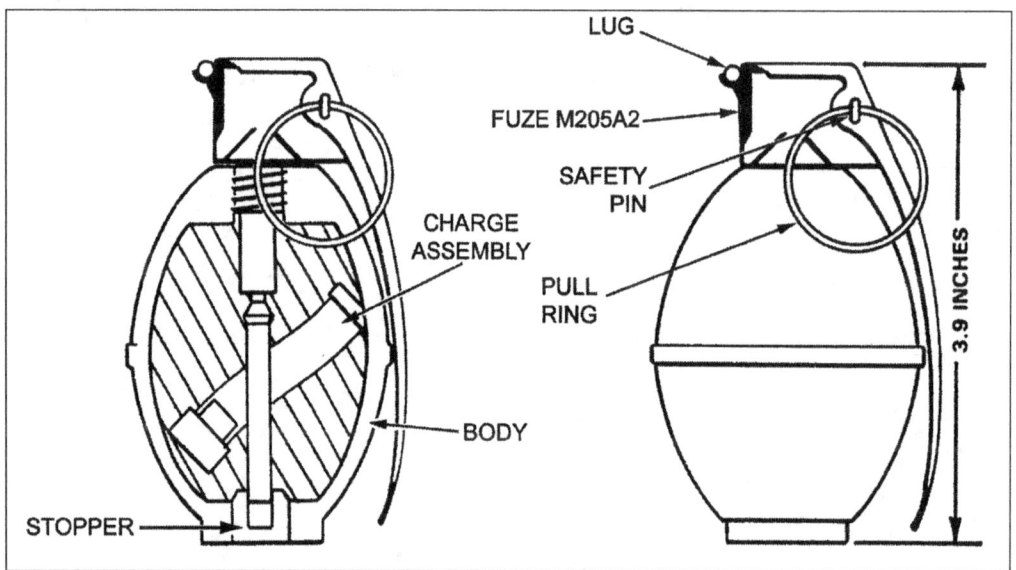

Figure E-1. M30 practice grenade.

E-2. MK1 ILLUMINATION HAND GRENADE

The MK1 illumination hand grenade (Figure E-2) is a ground signaling and ground pyrotechnic signal, except that the grenade burns only at ground level whereas pyrotechnic signals burn in flight or while suspended from a parachute. The MK1 should not be used in deep mud or swampy ground, which would result in little or no illumination. The grenade burns with a very hot flame and may be used as an incendiary agent. Because it is incendiary, soldiers should use caution to prevent fires that would be detrimental to tactical operations.

a. **Body**. The body of the MK1 illumination grenade is sheet metal.

b. **Filler**. The filler has 3.5 ounces of illuminating pyrotechnic composition.

c. **Fuze**. The fuze is a special igniter, which differs from other igniting type fuzes in that it contains a quick match rather than a powder delay train. The quick match has a burning time of 7 seconds, after which it sets off an igniter charge. The igniter charge initiates the burning process of the grenade's filler.

d. **Weight**. The grenade weighs 10 ounces.

e. **Capabilities**. The average soldier can throw the MK1 40 meters. The filler burns for 25 seconds, producing 55,000 candlepower and illuminating an area 200 meters in diameter.

f. **Color and Markings**. Older MK1 grenades are white with black markings; newer models are unpainted with black markings.

> **WARNING**
> Avoid looking directly at the illumination grenade as it burns, since the intensity of the light may damage the retina.

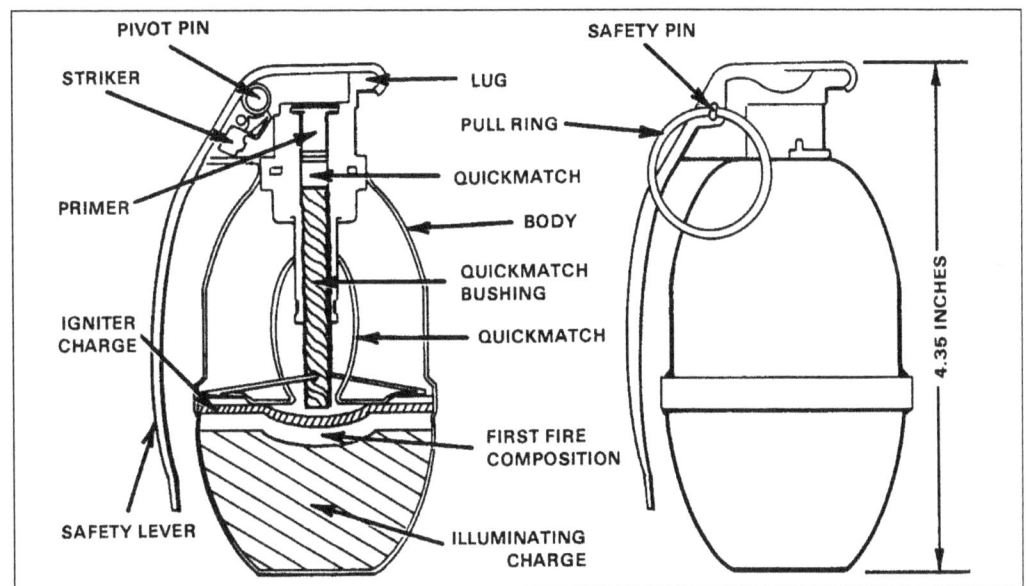

Figure E-2. MK1 illumination pyrotechnic hand grenade.

E-3. MK2 FRAGMENTATION HAND GRENADE

The MK2 (Figure E-3) is used to supplement small arms fire against the enemy in close combat. The grenade produces casualties by high-velocity projection of fragments.

    a. **Body**. The MK2 grenade body is cast iron.

    b. **Filler**. The filler has TNT, either flaked or granular.

    c. **Fuze**. The fuze is an M204A1 or M204A2.

    d. **Weight**. The grenade weighs 21 ounces.

    e. **Capabilities**. The average soldier can throw the grenade 30 meters. The MK2 grenade has a bursting radius of 10 meters.

    f. **Color and Markings**. The grenade has an olive drab body with a single yellow band, which indicates a high-explosive filler.

WARNING
If the fuze is loose, do not try to tighten it. This could set off the granular TNT in the grenade.

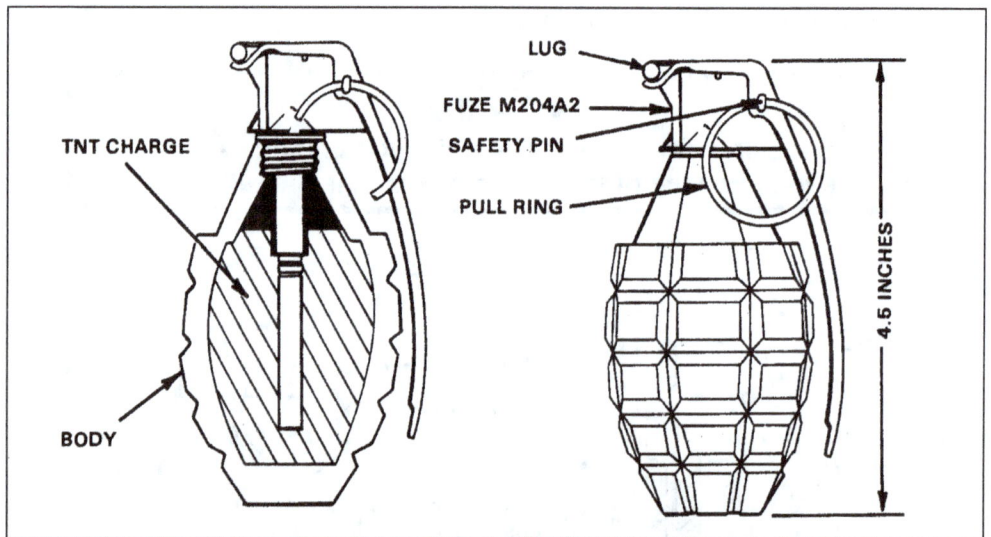

Figure E-3. MK2 fragmentation hand grenades.

E-4.   M26 AND M26A1 FRAGMENTATION HAND GRENADES

These grenades (Figure E-4) are used to supplement small arms fire against an enemy in close combat. They produce casualties through the high-velocity projection of fragments.

    a.   **Body**. The M26 and M26A1 grenade bodies are cast iron.

    b.   **Filler**. The fillers have TNT, either flaked or granular.

    c.   **Fuze**. The fuze is an M204A1 or M204A2.

    d.   **Weight**. Each grenade weighs 21 ounces.

    e.   **Capabilities**. The average soldier can throw these grenades 40 meters. They have an effective casualty radius of 15 meters.

    f.   **Color and Markings**. These grenades have an olive drab body with a single yellow band at the top and yellow markings, which indicate a high-explosive filler.

WARNING

Although the casualty-producing radius of the M26 grenade is 15 meters, fragments can disperse out to 230 meters.

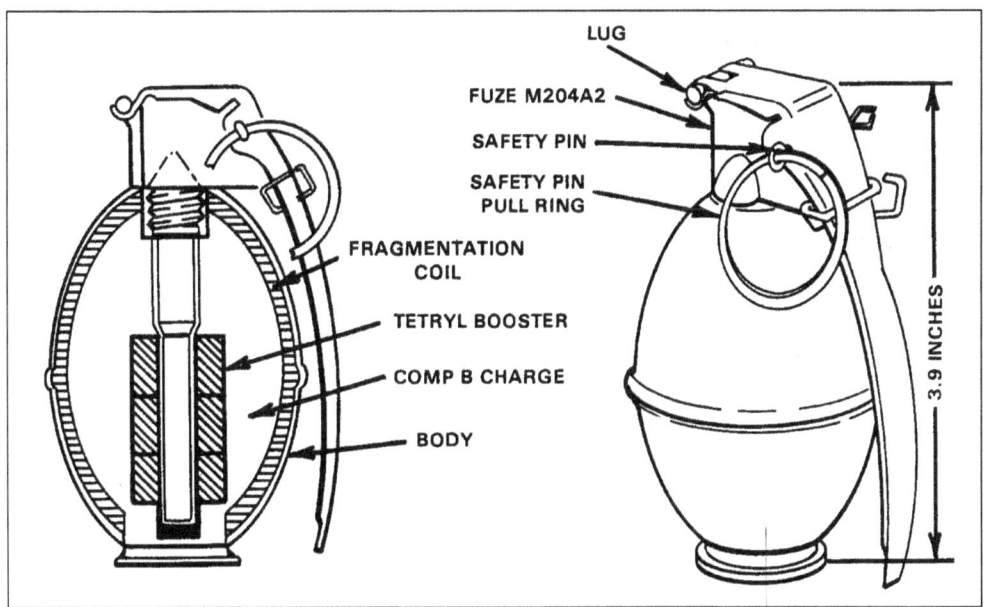

Figure E-4. M26 and M26A1 fragmentation hand grenade.

E-5. M7 AND M7A1 CN RIOT-CONTROL HAND GRENADES

The M7 and M7A1 grenades (Figure E-5) contain only CN (tear gas) filler. The two grenades differ in the amount of filler they contain.

a. **Body**. The M7 and M7A1 grenade bodies are sheet metal. The M7 has six emission holes at the top and two rows of nine emission holes each along the sides. The M7A1 has four emission holes at the top and one at the bottom.

b. **Filler**. The M7 grenade has 10.25 ounces of CN; the M7A1 has 12.5 ounces of CN.

c. **Fuze**. The fuze is an M201A1.

d. **Weight**. The M7 grenade weighs 17 ounces; the M7A1 weighs 18.5 ounces.

e. **Capabilities**. The average soldier can throw either grenade 35 meters. The grenades produce a dense cloud of irritant agent for 20 to 60 seconds.

f. **Color and Markings**. Each grenade has a gray body with a single red band and red markings.

WARNING
Friendly forces should don protective masks before using these grenades.

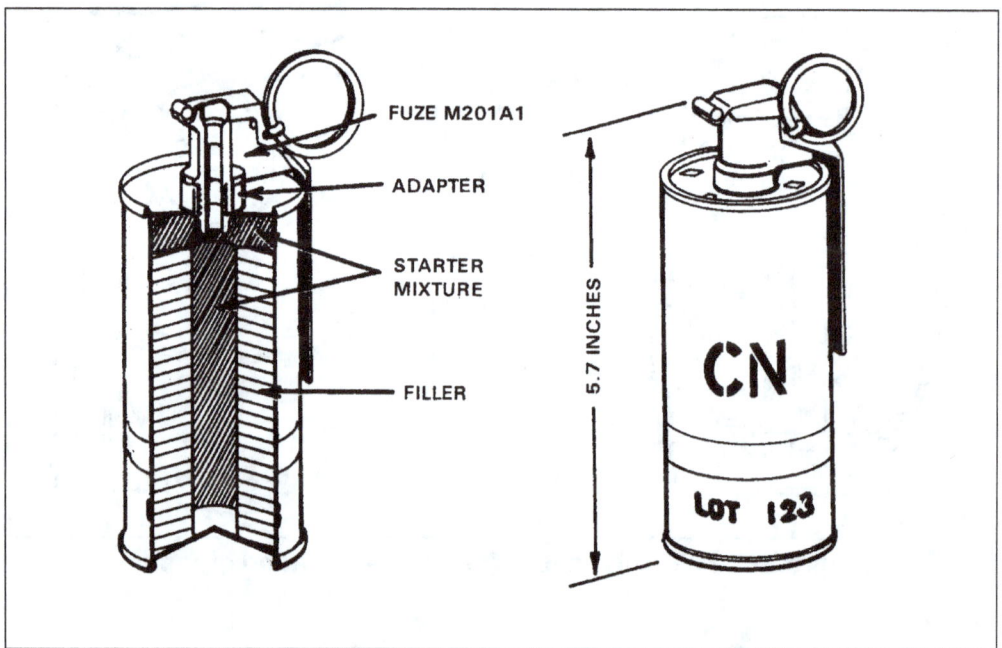

Figure E-5. M7 and M7A1 tear gas hand grenade.

E-6. M6 AND M6A1 CN-DM RIOT-CONTROL HAND GRENADES

The M6 and M6A1 grenades (Figure E 6) contain a combination mixture of CN and DM. They differ chiefly in external appearance and the manner in which the filler is combined.

a. **Body**. The M6 and M6A1 grenade bodies are sheet metal. The M6 has six emission holes at the top and two rows of nine emission holes each along the sides. The M6A1 has four emission holes at the top and one at the bottom.

b. **Filler**. The M6 grenade has 10.5 ounces of CN-DM mixture; the M6A1 has 9.5 ounces of CN-DM mixture.

c. **Fuze**. The fuze is an M201A1.

d. **Weight**. The M6 grenade weighs 17 ounces; the M6A1 weighs 20 ounces.

e. **Capabilities**. The average soldier can throw either grenade 35 meters. The grenades emit a dense cloud of irritant agent for 20 to 60 seconds

f. **Color and Markings**. These grenades have gray bodies with a single red band and red markings. (Under the standard color-coding system, the single red band and markings indicate nonpersistent riot-control filler. A double red band and markings indicate persistent riot-control filler, and any combination of green bands and markings indicates casualty-producing filler. Currently, there are no casualty-producing agents in hand grenade form.)

WARNING
Friendly forces should don protective masks before using these grenades.

Figure E-6. M6 and M6A1 riot-control hand grenade.

E-7. ABC-M25A1 AND ABC-M25A2 RIOT-CONTROL HAND GRENADES

The ABC riot-control hand grenade is a bursting munition with an integral fuze (Figure E-7). The M25A2 grenade is an improved version of the M25A1 grenade. The two types of grenades differ primarily in body construction. They are used to deliver all three types of riot-control agents presently used in hand grenades.

    a. **Body**. The body of this grenade is compressed fiber or plastic sphere.

    b. **Filler**. The fillers of the M25 series of riot-control hand grenades vary in weight and composition according to the type of agent contained in the grenade. All fillers are mixed with silica aerosol for increased dissemination efficiency.

    c. **Fuze**. The fuze type is integral.

    d. **Weight**. Each grenade weighs 7.5 to 8 ounces, depending on the type of filler.

    e. **Capabilities**. The average soldier can throw the grenade 50 meters. The M25 series of riot-control hand grenades have a radius burst (visible cloud grenade) of about 5 meters, but fragments of the grenade are occasionally projected up to 25 meters.

    f. **Color and Markings**. The color and markings are the same as the M6 and M6A1 grenades (paragraph E-6f). Most grenades of the M25 series currently in use are not painted according to any color-coding system. They are either totally unpainted or have only a red band and red markings.

WARNING
When the ABC-M25A1 grenade is employed, do not drop it because it may go off immediately. Do not attempt to replace a pulled safety pin and do not relax thumb pressure arming sleeve after the safety pin is pulled. Friendly forces should don protective masks before using these grenades.

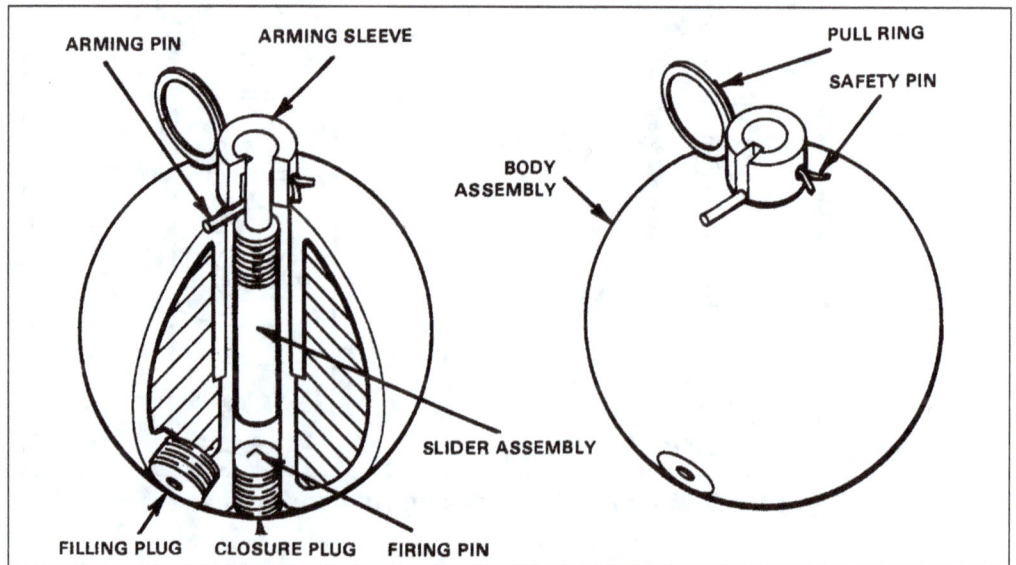

Figure E-7. The ABC-M25A1 riot-control hand grenade.

E-8. M34 WHITE PHOSPHORUS HAND GRENADE

The M34 chemical smoke grenade is the most versatile of all hand grenades (Figure E-8). The grenade can be used for signaling, screening, or incendiary missions, or for producing casualties. The use of this grenade also has a psychological impact on the enemy.

    a. **Body**. The M34 WP grenade body is compressed fiber or plastic sphere.

    b. **Filler**. The filler has 15 ounces of white phosphorous.

    c. **Fuze**. The fuze is an M206A2.

    d. **Weight**. The grenade weighs 27 ounces.

    e. **Capabilities**. The average soldier can throw the grenade 30 meters. The grenade has a bursting radius of 35 meters. All friendly personnel within this 35-meter area should be in a covered position to avoid being struck by burning particles. The WP filler burns for about 60 seconds at a temperature of 5,000 degrees Fahrenheit. This intense heat causes the smoke produced by the grenade to rise rapidly, especially in cool climates, making the M34 grenade less desirable for use as a screening agent. (The M15 WP smoke hand grenade is similar to the M34. For more information, refer to TM 9-1330-200-12.)

    f. **Color and Markings**. Under the old ammunition color-coding system, the white phosphorous grenade is light gray with a single yellow band and yellow markings. Under the new standard color-coding system, the M34 grenade is light green with a single yellow band and light red markings.

NOTE: Most M34 WP smoke hand grenades presently in use were manufactured before the standard color-coding system agreement and are painted according to the old color code.

WARNING
The M34 has a bursting radius of 35 meters, which is farther than the average soldier can throw it; therefore, the thrower must be in a covered or protected position.

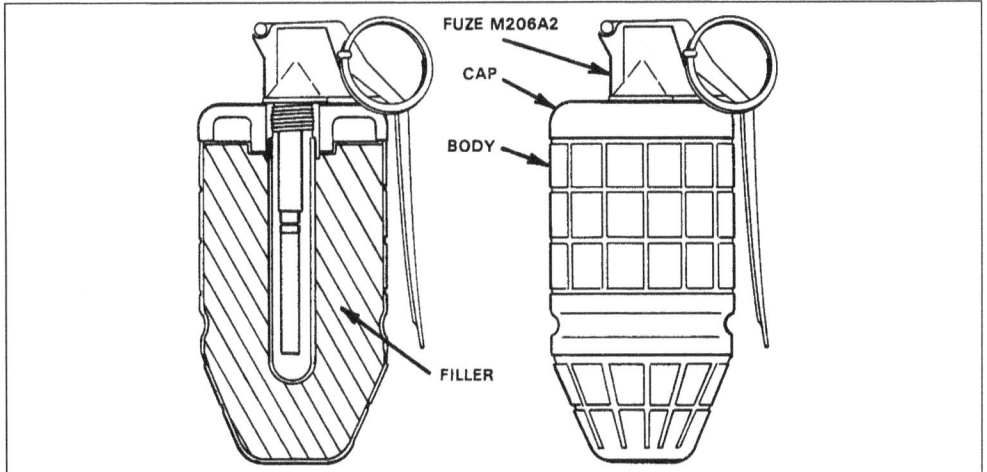

Figure E-8. M34 WP smoke hand grenade.

E-9. AN-M8 HC WHITE SMOKE

This grenade is used to produce dense clouds of white smoke for signaling and screening (Figure E-9).

    a. **Body**. The grenade body is a sheet steel cylinder.

    b. **Filler**. The filler has 19 ounces of Type C, HC smoke mixture.

    c. **Fuze**. The fuze is an M201A1.

    d. **Weight**. The grenade weighs 24 ounces.

    e. **Capabilities**. The average soldier can throw the AN-M8 30 meters. The grenade emits a dense cloud of white smoke for 105 to 150 seconds.

    f. **Color and Markings**. The grenade has a light green body with black markings and a white top.

WARNING

THE AN-M8 HAND GRENADE PRODUCES HARMFUL HYDROCHLORIC FUMES THAT IRRITATE THE EYES, THROAT, AND LUNGS. IT SHOULD NOT BE USED IN CLOSED-IN AREAS UNLESS SOLDIERS ARE WEARING PROTECTIVE MASKS.

WARNING

ANY DAMAGED AN-M8 HC GRENADES THAT EXPOSE THE FILLER ARE HAZARDOUS. EXPOSURE OF THE FILLER TO MOISTURE AND AIR COULD RESULT IN A CHEMICAL REACTION THAT WILL IGNITE THE GRENADE.

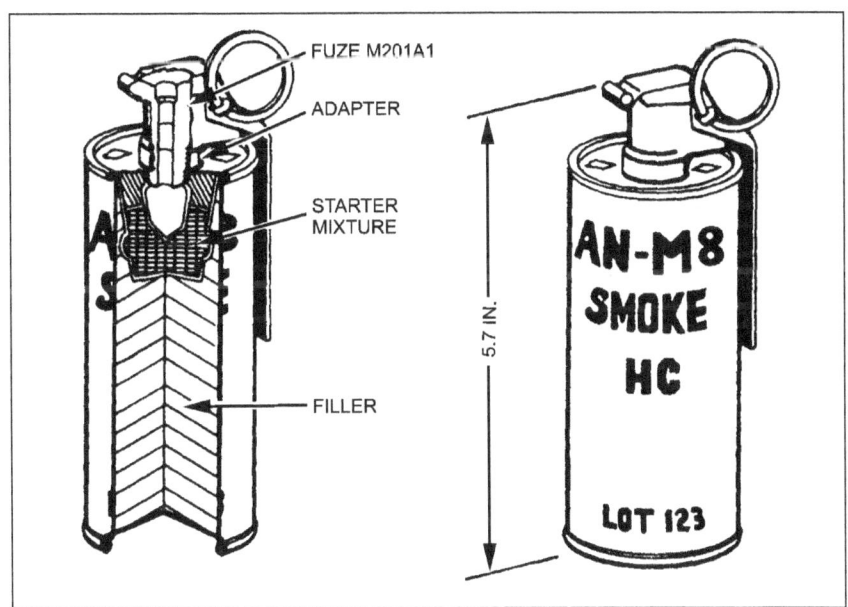

Figure E-9. AN-M8 HC white smoke grenade.

E-10. SAFETY CLIPS

Improvements have been made in safety clips. There are four types of safety clips that might be encountered on the obsolete grenades (Figure E-10).

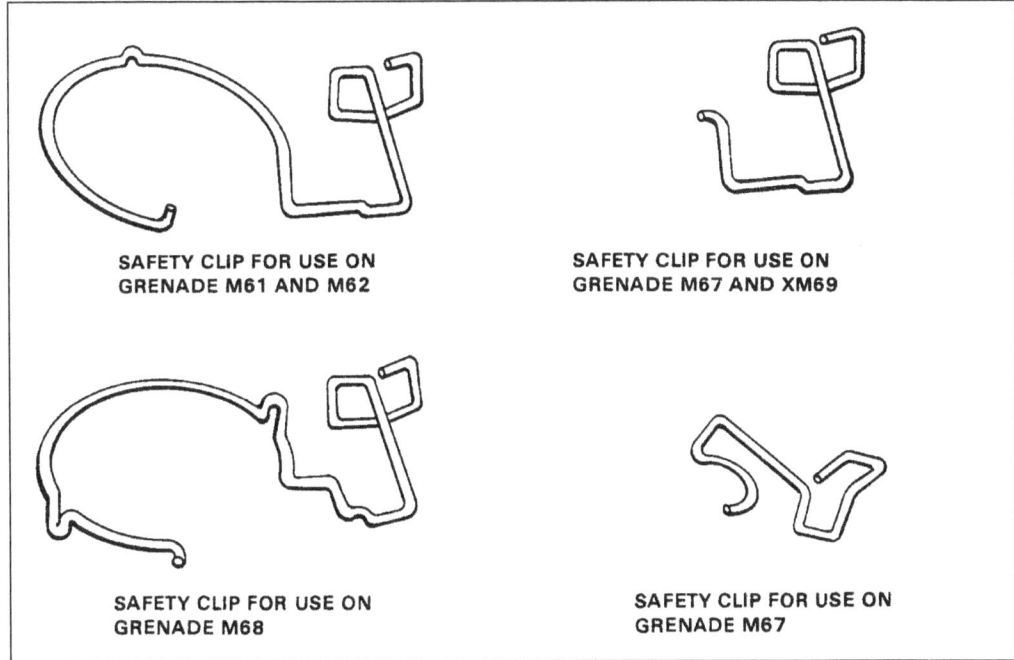

SAFETY CLIP FOR USE ON
GRENADE M61 AND M62

SAFETY CLIP FOR USE ON
GRENADE M67 AND XM69

SAFETY CLIP FOR USE ON
GRENADE M68

SAFETY CLIP FOR USE ON
GRENADE M67

Figure E-10. Safety clips on obsolete grenades.

APPENDIX F
NATO HAND GRENADES

This appendix provides general information on the identification, functions, and capabilities of NATO hand grenades. The North Atlantic Treaty Organization nations have an extensive inventory of grenades. This appendix describes only the more common grenades that the US soldier might encounter during joint operations.

Section I. NETHERLANDS

F-1.   NR17
- Type: Offensive. (Figure F-1)
- Weight: 475 grams.
- Length: 125 millimeters.
- Diameter: 56 millimeters.
- Body Material: Plastic.
- Fuze Type: Striker release.
- Filler Material: TNT.
- Filler Weight: 205 grams.
- Fuze Delay: 3-4 seconds.
- Effective Radius: 5 meters.
- Range Thrown: 30 to 40 meters.

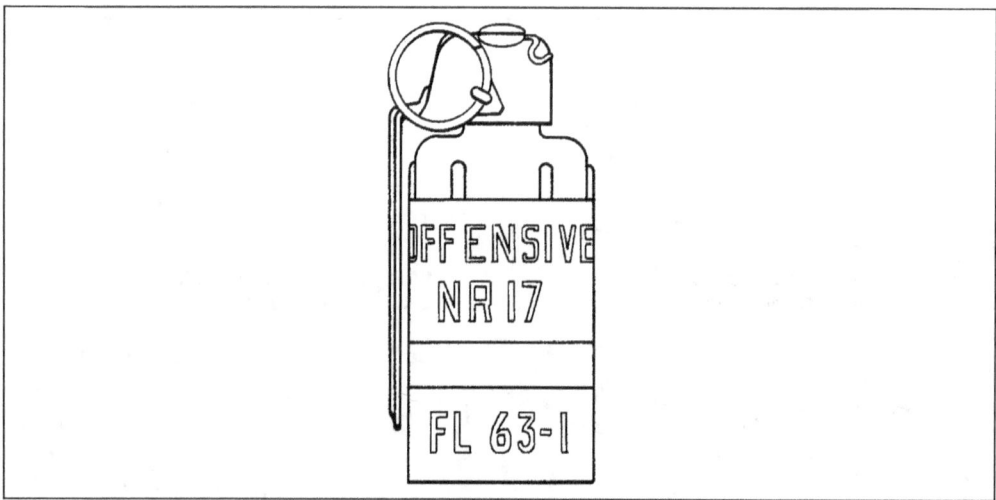

Figure F-1. NR17 hand grenade.

F-2. NR13C1

- Type: Fragmentation, offensive. (Figure F-2)
- Weight: 475 grams.
- Length: 143 millimeters.
- Diameter: 54 millimeters.
- Body Material: Steel.
- Filler Weight: 225 grams.
- Filler Material: High explosive.
- Fuze Type: Pyrotechnic delay.
- Fuze Delay: 5 seconds.
- Range Thrown: 30 meters.

Figure F-2. NR13C1 fragmentation hand grenade.

F-3. MARK 2

- Type: Fragmentation. (Figure F-3)
- Length: 114 millimeters.
- Diameter: 57 millimeters:
- Body Material: Cast iron.
- Filler Weight: 55 grams.
- Filler Material: TNT powdered.
- Fuze Type: Pyrotechnic delay.
- Fuze Delay: 3 seconds.

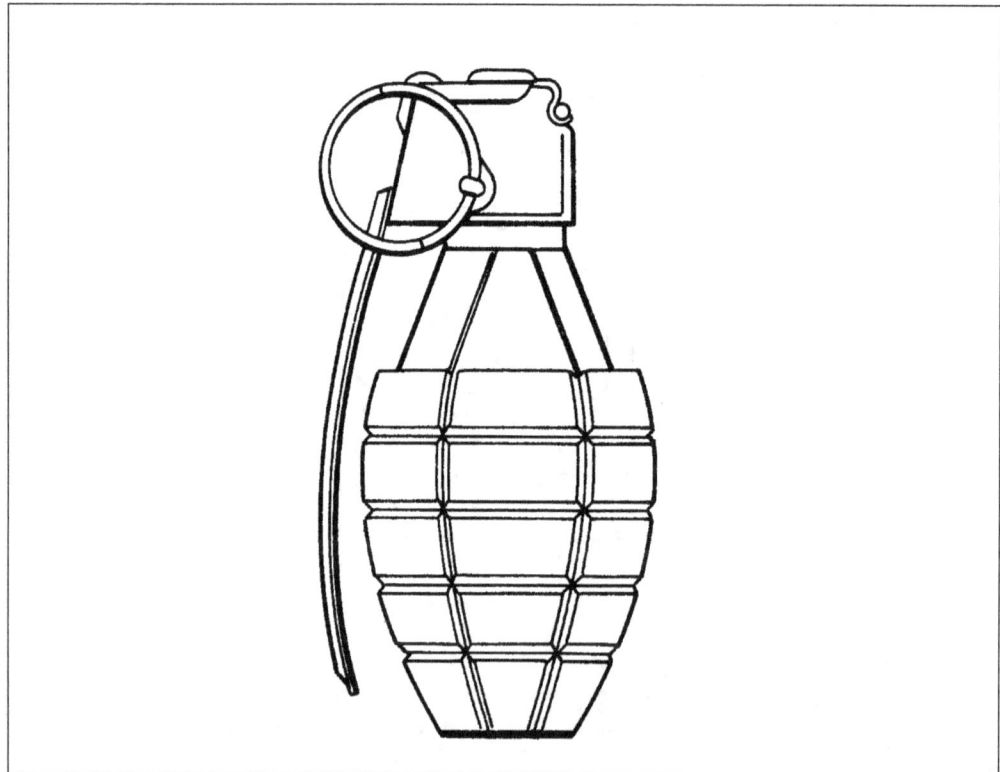

Figure F-3. Mark 2 fragmentation hand grenade.

F-4. NR1C1

- Type: Fragmentation. (Figure F-4)
- Weight: 670 grams.
- Length: 122 millimeters.
- Body Material: Cast iron.
- Filler Weight: 55 grams.
- Filler Material: TNT powdered.
- Fuze Type: Pyrotechnic delay.
- Fuze Delay: 3 seconds.

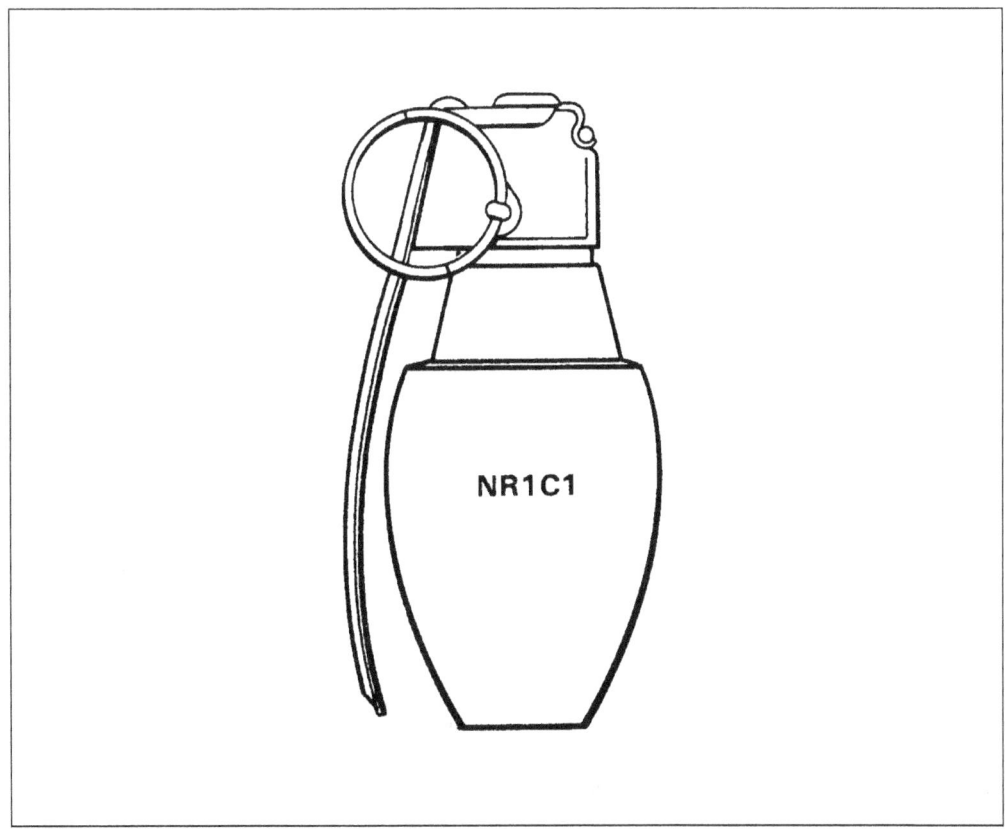

Figure F-4. NR1C1 fragmentation hand grenade.

F-5. **JNS 62-65**

- Type: Smoke. (Figure F-5)
- Weight: 660 grams.
- Length: 151 millimeters.
- Diameter: 63 millimeters.
- Body Material: Tinned steel.
- Filler Material: Colored smoke.
- Fuze Delay: 2 to 3 seconds.
- Burn Time: 1 to 2 minutes.

Figure F-5. JNS 62-65 smoke hand grenade.

F-6.   NR12
- Type: Incendiary. (Figure F-6)
- Weight: 820 grams.
- Length: 153 millimeters.
- Diameter: 63 millimeters.
- Body Material: Tinned steel.
- Filler Material: Thermite.
- Fuze Type: Striker release.
- Fuze Delay: 1 to 3 seconds.
- Range Thrown: 40 meters.
- Burn Time: 40 seconds.
- Peak Intensity: 2200°C

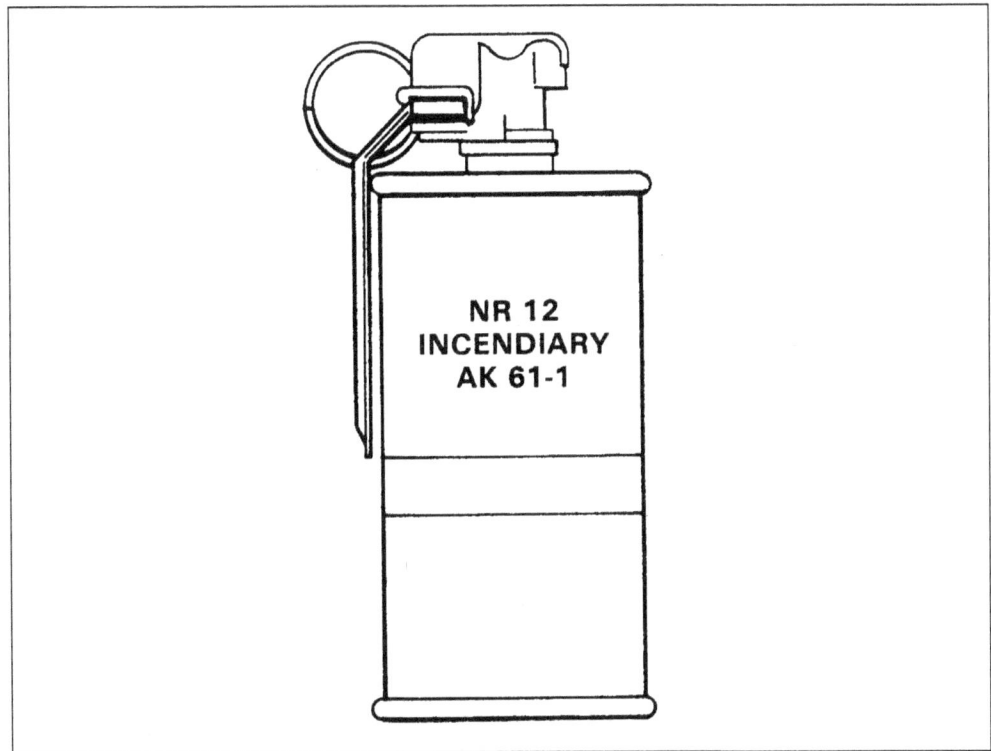

Figure F-6. NR12 incendiary hand grenade.

F-7.   NR16
- Type: Smoke. (Figure F-7)
- Weight: 284 grams.
- Length: 101 millimeters.
- Diameter: 50 millimeters.
- Body Material: Tinned Steel.
- Filler Material: White phosphorus.
- Fuze Type: Delay.
- Fuze Delay: 4 seconds.
- Range Thrown: 37 meters.

Figure F-7. NR16 smoke hand grenade.

F-8. NR20C1

- Type: Fragmentation. (Figure F-8)
- Weight: 390 grams.
- Length: 103 millimeters.
- Diameter: 60 millimeters.
- Body Material: Plastic.
- Filler Weight: 150 grams.
- Filler Material: Composition B.
- Fuze Type: Striker release.
- Fuze Delay: 3 to 4 seconds.
- Lethal Radius: 5 meters, safety range 15 to 20 meters.

Figure F-8. NR20C1 fragmentation hand grenade.

Section II. GERMANY

F-9.   DM 24/68

- Type: Incendiary smoke. (Figure F-9)
- Weight: 340 grams.
- Length: 133 millimeters.
- Diameter: 67 millimeters.
- Body Material: Plastic.
- Filler Weight: 255 grams.
- Filler Material. Red phosphorus.
- Fuze Type: Mechanical ignition.
- Fuze Delay: 2.5 seconds after ignition.
- Burn Time: 5 minutes.

Figure F-9. DM 24/68 incendiary hand grenade.

F-10. HC DM 15

- Type: Smoke. (Figure F-10)
- Weight: 1,200 grams.
- Length: 175 millimeters.
- Diameter: 76 millimeters.
- Body Material: Hexachlorethane.
- Fuze Type: Mechanical ignition.
- Fuze Delay: 2.5 seconds after ignition.
- Burn Time: 2.5 minutes.

Figure F-10. HC DM 15 smoke hand grenade.

F-11. M-DN 11

- Type: Fragmentation, defensive. (Figure F-11)
- Weight: 467 grams.
- Length: 97 millimeters.
- Diameter: 60 millimeters.
- Body Material: Plastic.
- Filler Weight: 43 grams, plasticized PETN.
- Fuze Type: Striker release.
- Fuze Delay: 3.5 to 4.5 seconds.

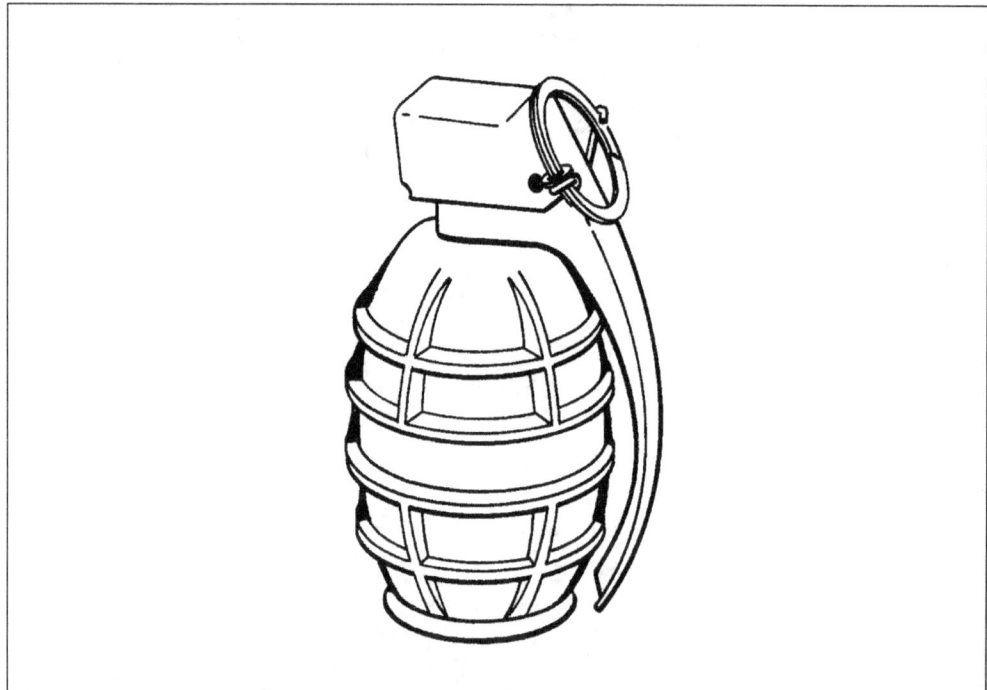

Figure F-11. M-DN 11 fragmentation hand grenade.

Section III. BELGIUM

F-12. 35X65 MECAR

- Type: Fragmentation, defensive. (Figure F-12)
- Weight: 230 grams.
- Length: 88 millimeters.
- Diameter: 35 millimeters.
- Body Material. Metal.
- Filler Material: Composition B.
- Fuze Type: Delay.
- Fuze Delay: 4 seconds.
- Range Thrown: 40 meters.
- Effective Radius: 10 meters.

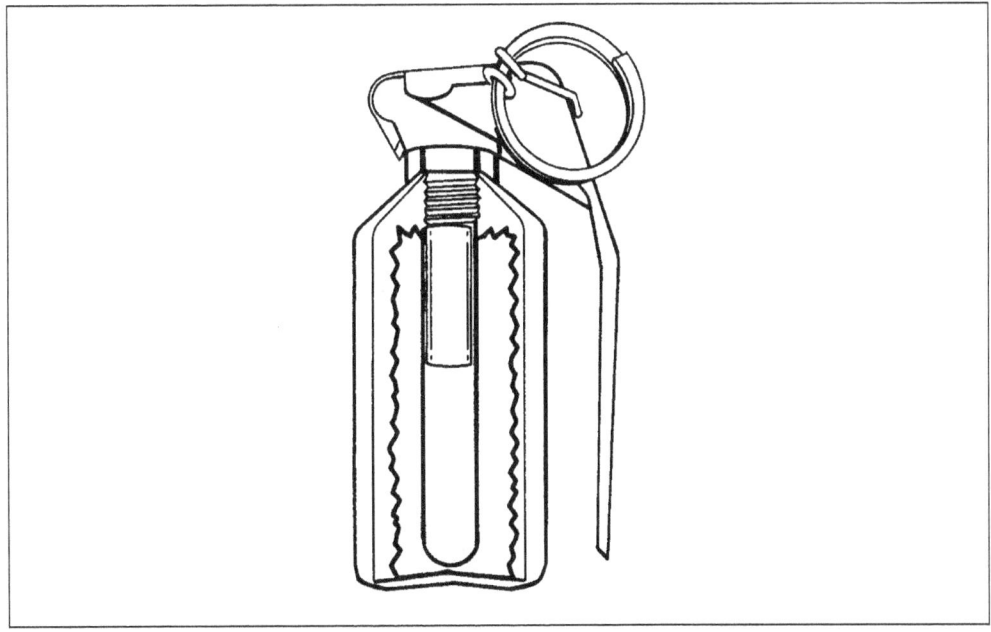

Figure F-12. 35X65 MECAR fragmentation hand grenade.

Section IV. UNITED KINGDOM

F-13. NO. 36M
- Type: Defensive. (Figure F-13)
- Weight: 600 grams.
- Length: 102 millimeters.
- Diameter: 60 millimeters.
- Body Material: Cast iron.
- Filler Weight: TNT, 60 grams.
- Fuze Type: Striker release.
- Fuze Delay: 3.5 to 4.5 seconds.
- Range Thrown: 25 meters.
- Effective Radius: 30 to 100 meters (40 fragments).

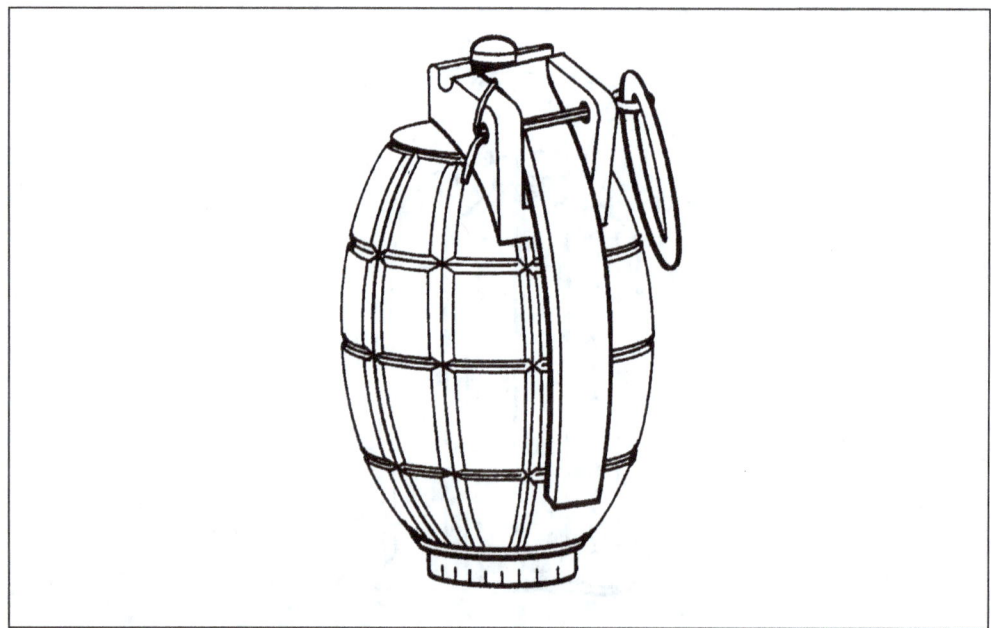

Figure F-13. No. 36M hand grenade.

F-14. PC1

- Type: Practice. (Figure F-14)
- Weight: 265 grams.
- Length: 95 millimeters.
- Diameter: 56 millimeters.
- Body Material: Soft plastic.
- Filler Weight: 80 grams.
- Filler Material: White powder.
- Fuze Type: Delay.
- Fuze Delay: 4.4 seconds + 0.5 seconds.
- Range Thrown: 40 meters.

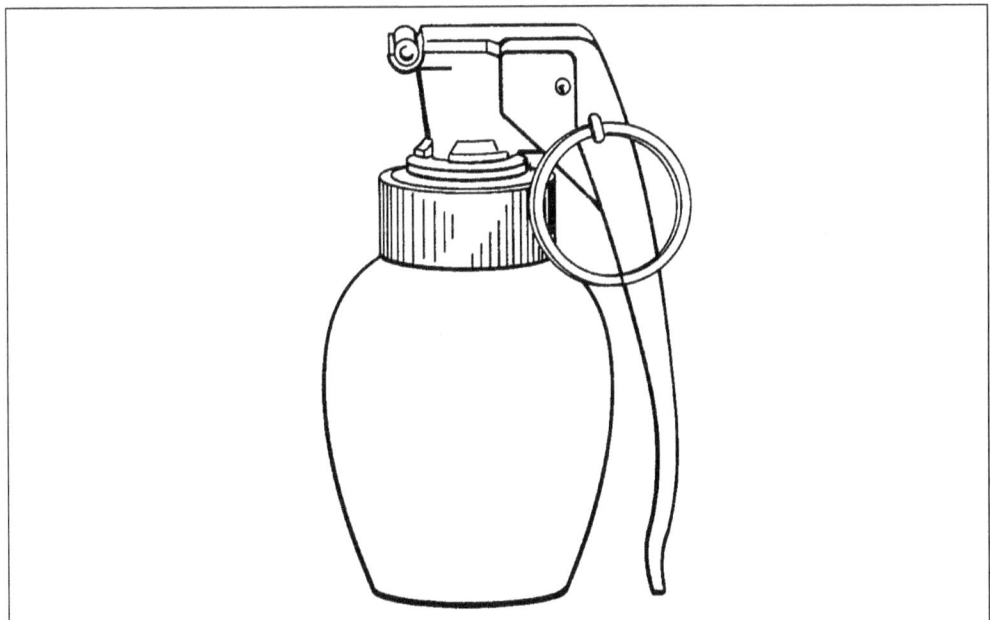

Figure F-14. PC1 practice hand grenade.

F-15. L2A2
- Type: Fragmentation. (Figure F-15)
- Weight: 395 grams.
- Length: 106 millimeters.
- Diameter: 60 millimeters.
- Body Material: Two-piece sheet-steel body with spiral wrapped fragmentation sleeve inside.
- Filler Material: RDX/TNT, 170 grams.
- Fuze Type: Striker release.
- Fuze Delay: 4 to 5 seconds.
- Range Thrown: 40 meters.
- Lethal Radius: 10 meters.

NOTE: Copy of US M26, being replaced by RO 01A1, a product improved model.

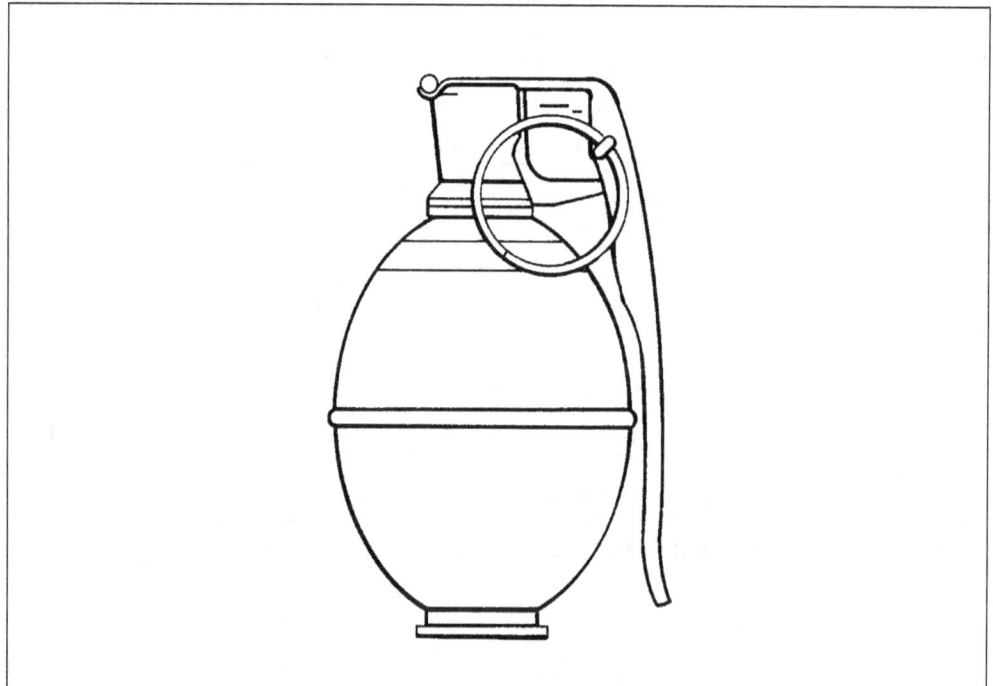

Figure F-15. L2A2 hand grenade.

F-16. NO. 83 N 201

- Type: Lachrymatory. (Figure F-16)
- Weight: 340 grams.
- Length: 135 millimeters.
- Diameter: 63 millimeters.
- Body Material: Tin.
- Filler Weight: 205 grams.
- Filler Material: CS, gas.
- Fuze Type: Striker release.
- Fuze Delay: 2 to 3 seconds.
- Range Thrown: 25 to 30 meters.
- Burn Time: About 25 seconds.

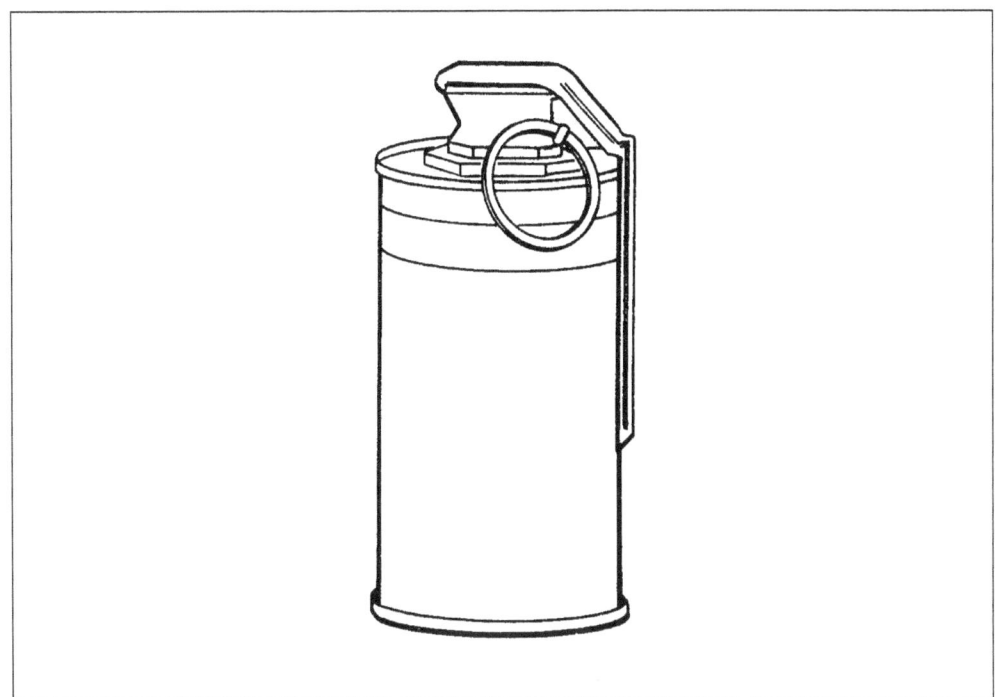

Figure F-16. No. 83 N 201 riot-control hand grenade.

F-17. RUBBER BURSTING CS

- Type: Riot control, L13A1 (N225 is similar). (Figure F-17)
- Weight: 550 Grams.
- Length: 175 millimeters.
- Diameter: 66 millimeters.
- Body Material: Rubber.
- Filler Weight: 470 grams.
- Filler Material: CS, 23 separate CS pellets.
- Fuze Type: Striker release.
- Fuze Delay: 2 to 2.4 seconds.
- Range Thrown: 25 to 35 meters.
- Burn Time: 12 seconds.
- Effective Radius: 15 meters.

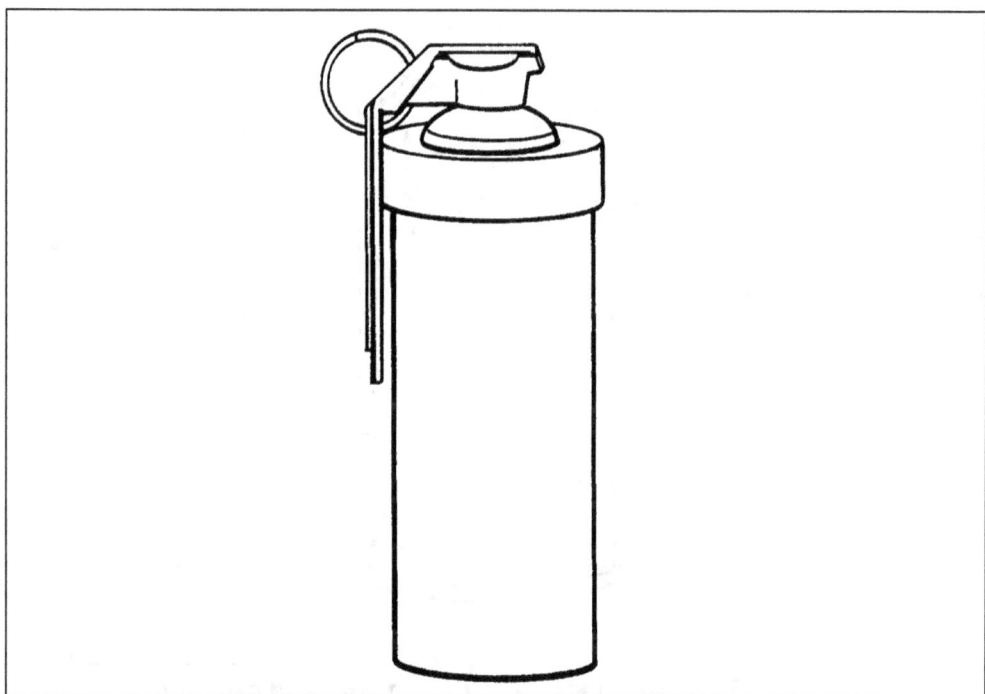

Figure F-17. Rubber bursting CS hand grenade.

Section V. AUSTRIA

F-18. SPL HGR 77
- Type: Defensive. (Figure F-18)
- Weight: 470 grams.
- Length: 96 millimeters.
- Diameter: 63 millimeters.
- Body Material: Rigid plastic.
- Filler Material: Plasticized PETN, 70 g.
- Fuze Type: Striker release.
- Fuze Delay: 3.5 to 4.5 seconds.
- Range Thrown: 45 meters.
- Effective Radius: 10 to 12 meters.

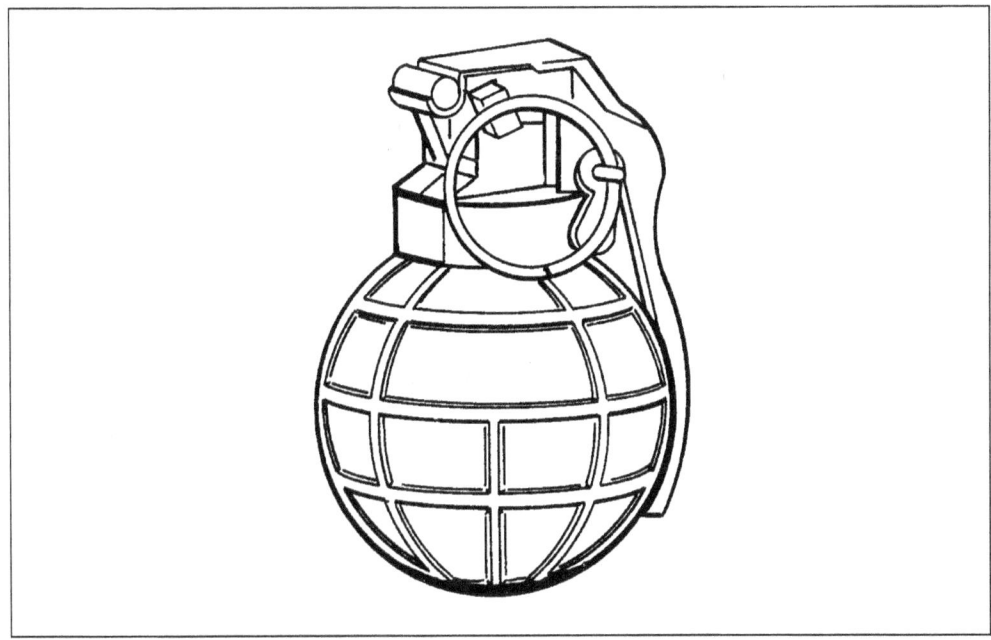

Figure F-18. Spl HGr 77 hand grenade.

F-19. HDGR 78

- Type: Defensive. (Figure F-19)
- Weight: 520 grams.
- Length: 115 millimeters.
- Diameter: 60 millimeters.
- Body Material: Plastic with steel pellets.
- Filler Weight: 70 grams.
- Filler Material: Plasticized PETN.
- Fuze Type: Striker release.
- Fuze Delay: 3 to 5 seconds.
- Range Thrown: 35 to 40 meters.
- Effective Radius: 10 meters.

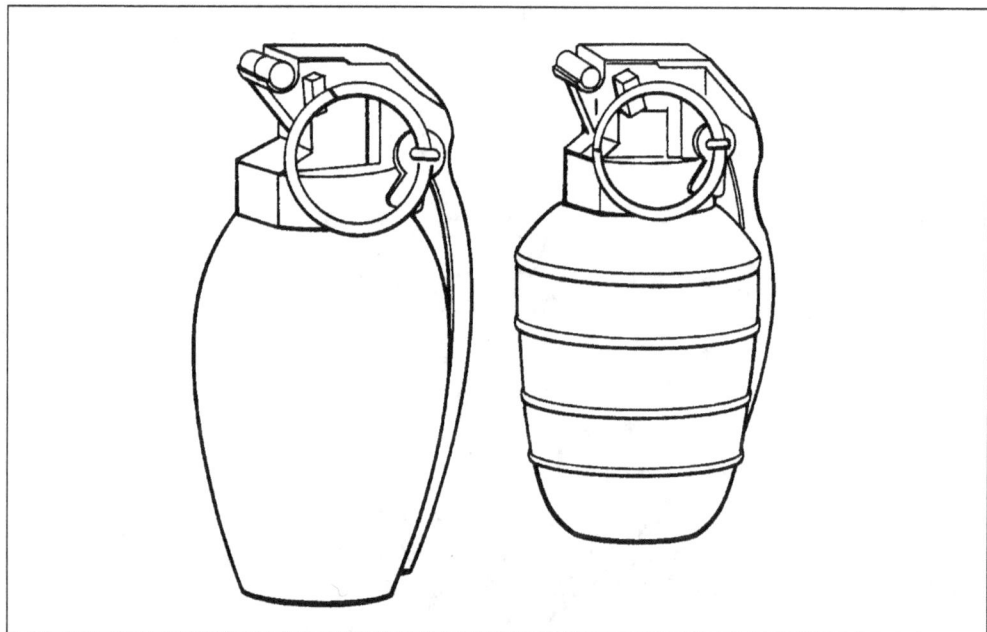

Figure F-19. HdGr 78 hand grenade.

F-20. HGR 79

- Type: Defensive. (Figure F-20)
- Weight: 370 grams.
- Length: 96 millimeters.
- Diameter: 58 millimeters.
- Body Material: Plastic.
- Filler Weight: 45 grams.
- Filler Material: Plasticized PETN.
- Fuze Type: Striker release.
- Fuze Delay: 3.5 to 4.5 seconds.
- Range Thrown: 45 meters.
- Effective Radius: 10 meters.

Figure F-20. HGr 79 hand grenade.

F-21. SPL HGR 84

- Type: Defensive. (Figure F-21)
- Weight: 490 grams.
- Length: 115 millimeters.
- Diameter: 61 millimeters.
- Body Material: Plastic.
- Filler Weight: 96 grams.
- Fuze Type: Striker release.
- Fuze Delay: 3.5 to 4.5 seconds nominal.
- Range Thrown: 35 to 40 meters.
- Effective Radius: 10 meters.

Figure F-21. Spl HGr 84 hand grenade.

F-22. HDGR 72

- Type: Defensive. (Figure F-22)
- Weight: 485 grams.
- Length: 115 millimeters.
- Diameter: 60 millimeter.
- Body Material: Rigid plastic.
- Filler Weight: 65 grams.
- Filler Material: Plasticized PETN.
- Fuze Type: Striker release.
- Fuze Delay: 3 to 5 seconds.
- Effective Radius: 10 meters.

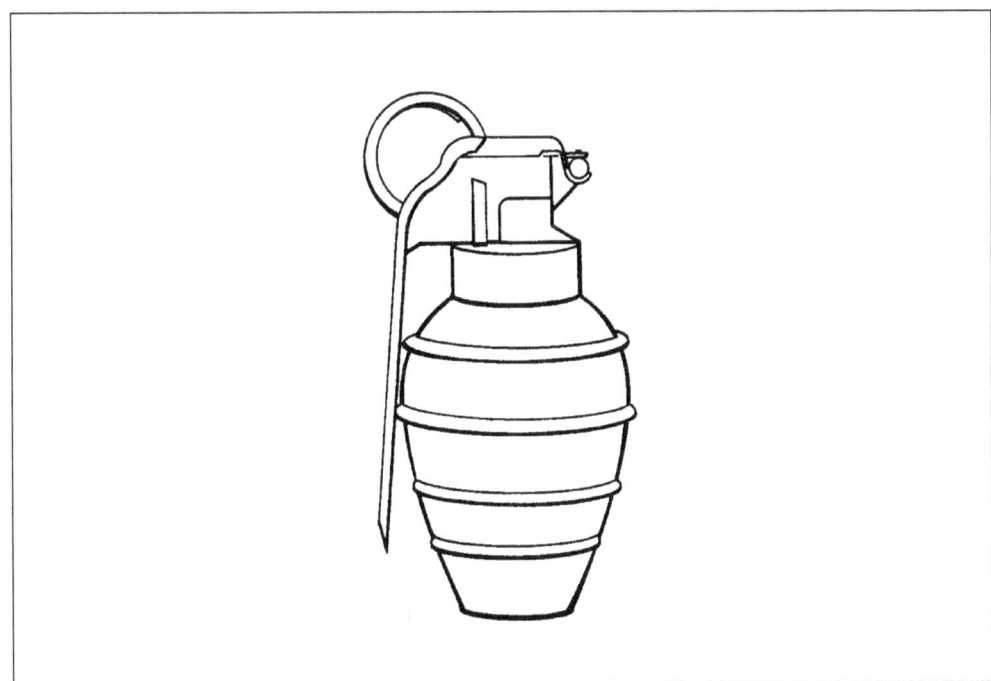

Figure F-22. HdGr 72 hand grenade.

F-23. HDGR 73

- Type: Defensive. (Figure F-23)
- Weight: 355 grams.
- Length: 91 millimeters.
- Diameter: 57 millimeters.
- Body Material: Plastic.
- Filler Weight: 37 grams.
- Filler Material: Plasticized PETN.
- Fuze Type: Striker release.
- Fuze Delay: 3 to 5 seconds.
- Effective Radius: 10 meters.

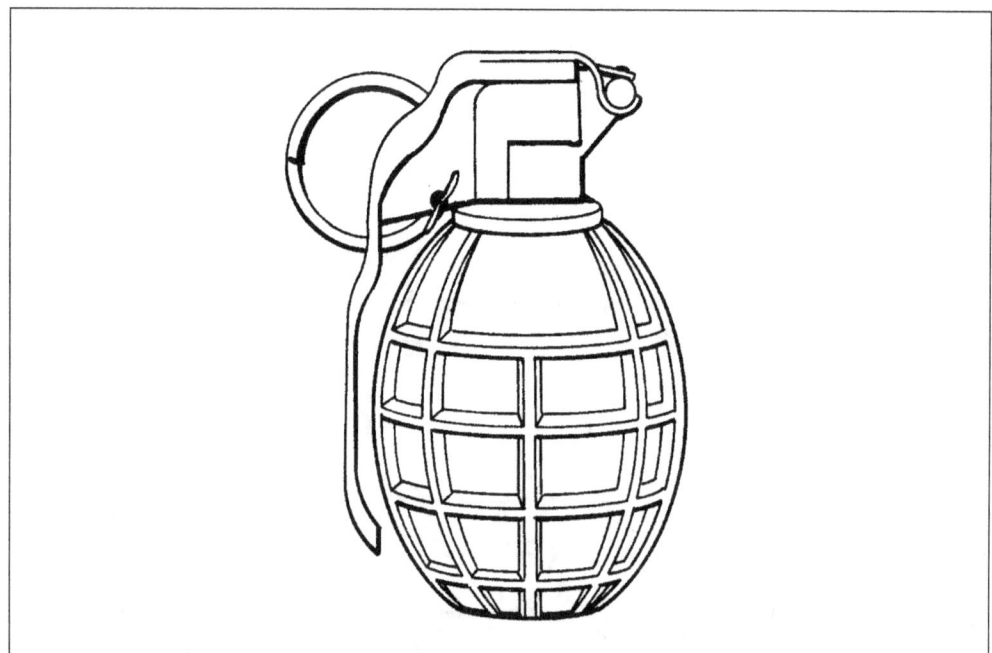

Figure F-23. HdGr 73 hand grenade.

REPRODUCIBLE FORMS

This appendix provides a blank copy of DA Form 3517-R, Hand Grenade Qualification Scorecard. This form is not available through normal supply channels. It may be reproduced locally on 8 1/2- x 11-inch paper.

HAND GRENADE QUALIFICATION SCORECARD
For use of this form, see FM 23-30. The proponent agency is TRADOC.

NOTE: In addition to the requirements on this scorecard, the soldier must throw two live fragmentation grenades to qualify.

A. DATE LIVE GRENADES WERE THROWN	B. INITIALS	
C. NAME *(Last, First, Middle Initial)*	D. DATE	
E. GRADE	F. SSN	G. UNIT

H. STATION	I. TYPE TARGET	J. GO	K. NO-GO	L. SCORER'S INITIALS
1	Engage Enemy from Fighting Position at a Range of 35 Meters *(Standing)*			
2	Engage Bunker			
3	Engage 82-mm Mortar Position at 20 Meters *(Kneeling)*			
4	Engage Enemy Behind Cover at 20 Meters *(Alternate Prone)*			
5	Engage Trench at 25 Meters *(Standing)*			
6	Engage Wheeled Vehicle at 25 Meters *(Kneeling)*			
7	Identify Hand Grenades			

M. QUALIFICATION STANDARD		CHECK
PASSED 7	EXPERT	
PASSED 6	FIRST CLASS	
PASSED 5	SECOND CLASS	
PASSED 4 OR LESS	UNQUALIFIED	

N. SIGNATURE OF SCORER/OIC

DA FORM 3517-R (Revised)　　　　　DA FORM 3517-R, NOV 88, IS OBSOLETE.

STATION 1. Engage Enemy from Fighting Position at a Range of 35 Meters (*Standing*)			STATION 5. Engage Trench at 25 Meters (*Standing*)		
PERFORMANCE MEASURES	GO	NO-GO	PERFORMANCE MEASURES	GO	NO-GO
A. Detonated at least one grenade within 5 meters of the center of target.			A. Detonated at least one grenade inside trench.		
B. Kept exposure time under 3 seconds.			B. Kept exposure time under 3 seconds.		
C. Returned to covered position after each throw.			C. Returned to covered position after each throw.		
D. Used proper grip.			D. Used proper grip.		
E. Used proper throwing techniques.			E. Used proper throwing techniques.		
F. Completed performance measures 1A through 1E within 15 seconds.			**STATION 6. Engage Wheeled Vehicle at 25 Meters (*Kneeling*)**		
STATION 2. Engage Bunker			A. Detonated within 1 meter of vehicle or within 5 meters of dismounting troops.		
A. Approached from blind side.			B. Kept exposure time under 3 seconds.		
B. Checked for bunker opening.			C. Returned to covered position after each throw.		
C. Detonated grenade in bunker.			D. Used proper grip.		
D. Rolled away from bunker.			E. Used proper throwing techniques.		
E. Used proper grip.			F. Completed performance measures 6A through 6E within 15 seconds.		
F. Use cook-off technique.			**STATION 7. Identify Hand Grenades**		
G. Completed performance measures 2A through 2E within 15 seconds.			A. Selected fragmentation grenade to engage enemy soldiers.		
STATION 3. Engage 82-mm Mortar Position at 20 Meters (*Kneeling*)			B. Identified M83 grenade as "White Smoke" or "HC smoke."		
A. Detonated at least one grenade inside mortar position.			C. Identified M18 grenade as "Colored Smoke" or "Purple (and so forth) Smoke." (*If specific color is stated, it must be the same color as on the training aid grenade used.*)		
B. Kept exposure time under 3 seconds.					
C. Returned to covered position after each throw.			D. Identified M7A2/A3 grenade as CS or riot control.		
D. Used proper grip.			E. Identified M14 grenades as incendiary.		
E. Used proper throwing techniques.					
F. Completed performance measures 3A through 3E within 15 seconds.			NOTES: 1. FOR PERFORMANCE MEASURES 7A THROUGH 7E, IF THE EXAMINEE CANNOT CORRECTLY STATE THE NAME OF THE GRENADE BUT CAN CORRECTLY IDENTIFY ITS USE, THEN THE EXAMINEE IS SCORED A "GO."		
STATION 4. Engage Enemy Behind Cover at 20 Meters (*Alternate Prone*)					
A. Detonated at least one grenade within 5 meters of the center of target.			2. EACH PERFORMANCE MEASURE AT EACH SECTION IS GRADED ON A PASS/FAIL STANDARD. A SOLDIER MUST PASS ALL OF THE STANDARDS TO RECEIVE A "GO" ON THAT STATION.		
B. Kept exposure time under 3 seconds.					
C. Returned to covered position after each throw.					
D. Used proper grip.					
E. Used proper throwing techniques.					
F. Completed performance measures 4A through 4E within 15 seconds.					

REVERSE OF DA FORM 3517-R (Revised)

GLOSSARY

ammo	ammunition
AR	automatic rifle; army regulation
ARTEP	Army Training and Evaluation Program
ASP	ammunition supply point
BFV	Bradley fighting vehicle
BMP	a fighting vehicle made by the former Soviet Union
BN	battalion
CN	tear gas
comp	composition
CS	tear gas; combat support
CSS	combat service support
CLP	cleaning, lubricant, petroleum
DA	Department of the Army
DM	vomiting gas
EOD	explosive ordnance disposal
ETLBV	enhanced tactical load-bearing vest
FM	field manual; frequency modulated
HC	hydrochloric
HG	hand grenade
HQ	headquarters
HGQC	hand grenade qualification course
IAW	in accordance with
LCE	load-carrying equipment
MBA	main battle area
METL	mission-essential task list
METT-T	mission, enemy, terrain, troops, and time
mm	millimeter
MOPP	mission-oriented protective posture
NATO	North Atlantic Treaty Organization
NCO	noncommissioned officer
NCOIC	noncommissioned officer in charge
NSN	national stock number

PETN	pentaerythritol tetranitrate
OD	olive drab
OIC	officer in charge
PA	public address
RATELO	radiotelephone operator
RDX	cyclonite
REGT	regiment
ROE	rules of engagement
RSO	range safety officer
STX	situational training exercise
SOI	signal operations instructions
SOP	standing operating procedure
TA	teraphthalic acid
TH	thermate
TM	technical manual
TNT	trinitrotoluene
TRADOC	Training and Doctrine Command
US	United States
WP	white phosphorous

REFERENCES

SOURCES USED
These are the sources quoted or paraphrased in this publication.

ARTEP 7-8 Drill   Battle Drills for the Infantry Rifle Platoon and Squad, 3 March 2000.

ARTEP 7-8 MTP   Mission Training Plan for the Infantry Rifle Platoon and Squad, 29 September 1994.

FM 3-100.4/   Environmental Considerations in Military Operations. 1 June 2000.
MCRP 4-11B

FM 7-7J   Mechanized Infantry Platoon and Squad (Bradley). 7 May 1993.

FM 7-8   Infantry Rifle Platoon and Squad. 22 April 1992.

TM 9-1330-200-12   Operator's and Organizational Maintenance Manual for Grenades. 17 September 1971; with Changes 1-15, dated 20 February 1976 through 16 June 1995.

TM 9-1370-206-10   Operator's Manual for Pyrotechnic Signals. 31 March 1991; with Change 1, 10 March 1992.

USAIC Reg 40-24   Prevention and First Aid Treatment of Cold Injury. 30 January 1989.

READINGS RECOMMENDED
These sources contain relevant supplemental information.

AR 385-63   Policies and Procedures for Firing Ammunition for Training, Target Practice and Combat. 15 October 1983.

FM 5-250   Explosives and Demolitions. 30 July 1998; with Change 1, 30 June 1999.

FM 21-11   First Aid for Soldiers. 27 October 1988; with Change 1, 28 August 1989, and Change 2, 4 December 1991.

TC 5-400   Unit Leaders' Handbook for Environmental Stewardship. 29 September 1994; with Changes 1-3, dated 3 October 1995 through 15 November 1999.

INTERNET WEB SITES
U.S. Army Publishing Agency: http://www.usapa.army.mil
Army Doctrine and Training Digital Library: http://www.adtdl.army.mil

HAND GRENADE QUALIFICATION SCORECARD
For use of this form, see FM 23-30. The proponent agency is TRADOC.

NOTE: In addition to the requirements on this scorecard, the soldier must throw two live fragmentation grenades to qualify.

A. DATE LIVE GRENADES WERE THROWN		B. INITIALS		
C. NAME (*Last, First, Middle Initial*)		D. DATE		
E. GRADE	F. SSN	G. UNIT		

H. STATION	I. TYPE TARGET	J. GO	K. NO-GO	L. SCORER'S INITIALS
1	**Engage Enemy from Fighting Position at a Range of 35 Meters** (*Standing*)			
2	**Engage Bunker**			
3	**Engage 82-mm Mortar Position at 20 Meters** (*Kneeling*)			
4	**Engage Enemy Behind Cover at 20 Meters** (*Alternate Prone*)			
5	**Engage Trench at 25 Meters** (*Standing*)			
6	**Engage Wheeled Vehicle at 25 Meters** (*Kneeling*)			
7	**Identify Hand Grenades**			

M. QUALIFICATION STANDARD		
		CHECK
PASSED 7	EXPERT	
PASSED 6	FIRST CLASS	
PASSED 5	SECOND CLASS	
PASSED 4 OR LESS	UNQUALIFIED	

N. SIGNATURE OF SCORER/OIC

DA FORM 3517-R (Revised)   DA FORM 3517-R, NOV 88, IS OBSOLETE.

STATION 1. Engage Enemy from Fighting Position at a Range of 35 Meters *(Standing)*			STATION 5. Engage Trench at 25 Meters *(Standing)*		
PERFORMANCE MEASURES	GO	NO-GO	PERFORMANCE MEASURES	GO	NO-GO
A. Detonated at least one grenade within 5 meters of the center of target.			A. Detonated at least one grenade inside trench.		
B. Kept exposure time under 3 seconds.			B. Kept exposure time under 3 seconds.		
C. Returned to covered position after each throw.			C. Returned to covered position after each throw.		
D. Used proper grip.			D. Used proper grip.		
E. Used proper throwing techniques.			E. Used proper throwing techniques.		
F. Completed performance measures 1A through 1E within 15 seconds.			STATION 6. Engage Wheeled Vehicle at 25 Meters *(Kneeling)*		
STATION 2. Engage Bunker			A. Detonated within 1 meter of vehicle or within 5 meters of dismounting troops.		
A. Approached from blind side.			B. Kept exposure time under 3 seconds.		
B. Checked for bunker opening.			C. Returned to covered position after each throw.		
C. Detonated grenade in bunker.			D. Used proper grip.		
D. Rolled away from bunker.			E. Used proper throwing techniques.		
E. Used proper grip.			F. Completed performance measures 6A through 6E within 15 seconds.		
F. Use cook-off technique.			**STATION 7. Identify Hand Grenades**		
G. Completed performance measures 2A through 2E within 15 seconds.			A. Selected fragmentation grenade to engage enemy soldiers.		
STATION 3. Engage 82-mm Mortar Position at 20 Meters *(Kneeling)*			B. Identified M83 grenade as "White Smoke" or "HC smoke."		
A. Detonated at least one grenade inside mortar position.			C. Identified M18 grenade as "Colored Smoke" or "Purple (and so forth) Smoke." *(If specific color is stated, it must be the same color as on the training aid grenade used.)*		
B. Kept exposure time under 3 seconds.					
C. Returned to covered position after each throw.			D. Identified M7A2/A3 grenade as CS or riot control.		
D. Used proper grip.			E. Identified M14 grenades as incendiary.		
E. Used proper throwing techniques.					
F. Completed performance measures 3A through 3E within 15 seconds.			NOTES: 1. FOR PERFORMANCE MEASURES 7A THROUGH 7E, IF THE EXAMINEE CANNOT CORRECTLY STATE THE NAME OF THE GRENADE BUT CAN CORRECTLY IDENTIFY ITS USE, THEN THE EXAMINEE IS SCORED A "GO."		
STATION 4. Engage Enemy Behind Cover at 20 Meters *(Alternate Prone)*					
A. Detonated at least one grenade within 5 meters of the center of target.			2. EACH PERFORMANCE MEASURE AT EACH SECTION IS GRADED ON A PASS/FAIL STANDARD. A SOLDIER MUST PASS ALL OF THE STANDARDS TO RECEIVE A "GO" ON THAT STATION.		
B. Kept exposure time under 3 seconds.					
C. Returned to covered position after each throw.					
D. Used proper grip.					
E. Used proper throwing techniques.					
F. Completed performance measures 4A through 4E within 15 seconds.					

REVERSE OF DA FORM 3517-R (Revised)

By Order of the Secretary of the Army:

ERIC K. SHINSEKI
General, United States Army
Chief of Staff

Official:

JOEL B. HUDSON
Administrative Assistant to the
Secretary of the Army
0021503

DISTRIBUTION:

Active Army, Army National Guard, and U. S. Army Reserve: To be distributed in accordance with the initial distribution number 110196, requirements for FM 3-23.30.

PIN: 078392-000